THE ULTIMATE PLAYDATE GUIDE

How to Build Connections, Friendships, and Social Skills

Janine Halloran, LMHC

THE ULTIMATE PLAYDATE GUIDE

For information contact:
Encourage Play, LLC
288 Grove Street #321
Braintree, MA 02184
http://www.encourageplay.com

Book Editing by Amy Maranville, Kraken Communications
Book Formatting by Derek Murphy @Creativindie
Cover design by Encourage Play, LLC
ISBN: 978-1-7333871-1-8

First Edition: August 2019
10 9 8 7 6 5 4 3 2 1

About the Author

Janine Halloran is a Licensed Mental Health Counselor who has been working with children, teens, and their families for over 15 years. She has been helping children and teens build their social skills using play throughout her career in a variety of settings, including schools, social skills groups, and summer programs.

She is the Founder of Encourage Play, LLC, and is the author of Social Skills for Kids: Over 75 Fun Games & Activities for Building Better Relationships, Problem Solving & Improving Communication. Her work has been featured in the Washington Post, Boston Globe, Huffington Post, NBC Parent Toolkit, and The Skimm® Newsletter. She was named Skimm'r® of the Year in 2018.

She is also the founder of Coping Skills for Kids, and the author of the #1 Bestselling Coping Skills for Kids Workbook. In 2019, Janine started the Calm & Connected podcast with quick ideas for social skills, coping skills and self-care. Janine lives in Massachusetts with her husband and two children.

Dedication

This book is dedicated to my two children, Elisa and Noah.

Thank you for always being willing to play and try my wacky

ideas. Over the years, you've taught me so much about

playdates, and what I've learned from you has made it possible

for me to write this book. Thanks for being awesome!

"My magic is never giving up!"

TABLE OF CONTENTS

Page Numbers, Best Location, Mess Level, & Age Range for Activities

Playdate Activities	Page #	Location	Messiness	Age
CREATIVE PLAY	27			
Make a Paper Cup Tower	28	🏠	❁	3 and up
Have Fun with Water Beads	30	🏠 🌳	❁ ❁	3 and up
Build Tents and Forts	32	🏠	❁ ❁	3 and up
Play in Sand Trays	34	🌳	❁ ❁ ❁	3 and up
Draw Pictures	36	🏠	❁ ❁	3 and up
Use Some Sidewalk Chalk	38	🌳	❁ ❁	3 and up
Play with Magic Nuudles®	40	🏠 🌳	❁ ❁	3 and up
Be Creative with Sunprints®	42	🌳	❁ ❁	3 and up
Create Art Using Nature	44	🏠 🌳	❁ ❁	3 and up
Build a Fairy Garden	46	🏠 🌳	❁ ❁	3 and up
Put on a Puppet Show	48	🏠	❁	3 and up
Paint with Q-Tips	50	🏠 🌳	❁ ❁ ❁	3 and up
Paint Rocks	52	🏠 🌳	❁ ❁ ❁	3 and up
Paint with Salt	54	🏠 🌳	❁ ❁ ❁	3 and up

INTRODUCTION

More and more research confirms that **play is the best way for children to learn and communicate.** Through play, children figure out how to interact with one another, problem solve, make decisions, collaborate, and work together as a team.

As a therapist, I have also seen the power of play first hand. When I was first starting out as a therapist, I wanted to work with elementary-school-aged kids, and I was excited to start my internship with that age group. When I met with those younger clients during those first few weeks, things didn't go as I expected – the kids didn't say much of anything and it didn't seem like I was going to get anywhere fast. I went to my supervisor, perplexed about what was going wrong. He said, "You need to get down on the floor and play with them."

When you play a game with a child, it makes it much easier for them to get comfortable and open up to you about what's going on for them. Once I started playing, my young clients started to open up and talk about what was happening. By using play as our method of communicating, I was able to understand what was happening for them, and speak with them about trying different, healthier strategies to help manage their challenges.

The same can be said for child-to-child communication. When your child struggles socially, it can be so difficult for them to communicate feelings or frustrations to other children. Helping your child to choose a successful activity during a playdate can make all the difference in helping them connect and bond with a friend.

Throughout my career, the power of play has presented itself again and again as a crucial component of successful interactions with (and between) children. Whether I'm working with children in schools, small groups, after school programs, or in private practice, I continue to use structured and unstructured activities like the ones in this book. It's incredible how much children can learn and communicate through play!

What Counts as Play?

What is play exactly? A definition of play I often use is "to engage in activity for enjoyment and recreation rather than a serious or practical purpose."

One thing that can be confusing about the definition of play is what one person considers play may not be play for another. In my own family, my husband and daughter find it quite enjoyable to go on roller coasters, whereas my son and I find them awful. Riding roller coasters is play for them, and misery for us. Some people love playing board games, while others love drawing, and others love running. All of these could be considered play.

To more clearly define the variety of ways children can play, researchers and experts have been categorizing play into what's known as **play types.** I personally like the play types described by Bob Hughes, a researcher and playworker in the UK. Hughes sets up and arranges play spaces designed for children to use after school and during vacations. He has published several works about play, but my favorite is his "Taxonomy of 16 Play Types," in which he identifies 16 distinct types of play he has seen over the years in his work with children and in his research. I find that it's the most thorough explanation of all the different ways children can play.

16 Play Types

Symbolic Play

Using objects, or actions to represent other objects, actions, or ideas, e.g. using a cardboard tube like a telescope.

Rough and Tumble Play

Discovering physical flexibility, generally friendly and positive.

Socio-Dramatic Play

When children act out experiences, e.g. playing house

Creative Play

Allows children to explore, try out new ideas and use their imagination.

Social Play

Any social situation where it's expected that everyone will follow the set rules - like during a game

Communication Play

Play using words, gestures e.g. charades, telling jokes, play acting, etc.

Dramatic Play

Play where children figure out roles to play, assign them and then act them out.

Locomotor Play

Movement for movement's sake, just because it's fun. Things like chase, tag, hide and seek and tree climbing

Imaginative Play

play where the conventional rules, which govern the physical world, do not apply, like imagining you are a bee, or pretending you have wings.

Exploratory Play

using senses of smell, touch and even taste to explore and discover the texture and function of things around them

Fantasy Play

child's imagination gets to run wild and they get to play out things that are that are unlikely to occur, like being a pilot or driving a car.

Deep Play

Play which allows the child to encounter risky experiences and conquer fear like heights, snakes, and creepy crawlies

Mastery Play

control of the physical and affective ingredients of the environments, like digging holes or constructing shelters.

Object Play

play which uses sequences of hand-eye manipulations and movements, like using a paintbrush.

Role Play

play exploring ways of being, although not normally of an intense nature, like brushing with a broom, dialing with a telephone..

Recapitulative Play

play that allows the child to explore ancestry, history, rituals, stories, rhymes, fire and darkness.

Play Type Information from Hughes, B. (2002) A Playworker's Taxonomy of Play Types, 2nd edition, London: PlayLink.

A Quick Note: One thing to keep in mind is that one playtime can encompass several play types. For example, if children are playing pirates, they could be using rough and tumble play, symbolic play, dramatic play, communication play, social play, fantasy play, and imaginative play!

Why Play Matters

Play can and should be part of our everyday lives. Play is fun, relaxing and enjoyable but it's also important. Play is so important that it's even part of the United Nations Convention on the Rights of the Child (1996). Article 31 states that children have the right "to engage in play and recreational activities."

Play is a child's natural language. It's how they communicate their thoughts and feelings about what's going on in their world. Children learn about self-regulation and managing their feelings through play. Through play, children also learn how to interact with others, and understand the impact their behavior may have on other people, and how other people impact them, developing their empathy and understanding.

Play is not just fun, it's also essential. Dr. Stuart Brown talks about a lack of play being similar to a lack of sleep. Just as all humans need to sleep, they also need time to play.

Play can help children reset and re-energize. Children can focus more after a brain and body break.

Through play, children practice and learn essential skills for life. In the book Purposeful Play, three elementary school teachers talk about the power play has in preparing children for the future: "Play gives children exactly what they need now, which will help them develop into the kinds of people who can handle what comes next."

Why Kids Struggle with Play

As individuals, we all develop at different times. When it comes to play, it's no different. There are children who play easily with others naturally, and there are those who need explicit directions to learn those skills. Children develop different skills at different times and that is a normal and expected part of child development.

When your child is having difficulty with play, it doesn't mean that they have an undiagnosed disorder, that there is something wrong, or that you did something wrong. We all develop at different paces over time. We can support our children by encouraging play, and supporting them and directing them when they need it.

If you are concerned about delays you are seeing in your child related to play, social interaction, speech, sensory, movement, or other milestones, I would encourage you to start first by speaking with your pediatrician to get their opinion on what you are seeing. They can then advise you if you need to take any follow up steps, make appointments with a more specialized medical professional, or let you know if they think additional evaluations makes sense.

For those of you who already have a child who has been diagnosed with Autism, ADHD, a developmental delay, etc., they may struggle with play and interacting with others. I want you to know that play matters and makes a difference for all children. Play is a powerful way to teach any child skills. It may not be linear or smooth, and that's OK. In fact, play can help those children who need additional support and scaffolding by allowing children to practice and review these skills in a more enjoyable playful manner.

Social Development and Play

As children develop and grow, so does their way of interacting socially. Let's take a brief look at how social play develops and changes over time. Mildred Parten did research on children's play, and noted six stages that children go through, starting at birth.

1. Unoccupied play – Infants engage in random movements with seemingly no apparent purpose. This is the beginning of play!

<u>Age Range</u>: birth +

Examples of Unoccupied Play: grabbing things, swatting at things, following things with your eyes, babbling, moving arms and legs, putting feet in mouth

How You Can Help / Interact: Use high contrast toys with babies (for example, black and white) because babies eyes can more easily register the differences in high contrast items. Offer different sensory experiences like setting out different baby safe fabrics during tummy time. Talk and interact to encourage the start of communication. Did you know some babies as young as a few days old can mimic you sticking out your tongue? Try it, it's fun!

2. Solitary play – This is when children start to play on their own. When engaged in solitary play, children do not seem to notice other kids sitting or playing nearby during this type of play.

Age Range: 1 year + (all age groups can and should have some time for independent play)

Examples of Solitary Play: building with blocks, doing a puzzle, drawing, reading a book

How You Can Help: Encourage independent play for short amounts of time beginning when kids are about one year old. Set a timer and have them play independently just for a few minutes. As they get older, increase the time.

3. Onlooker play – The next stage of play is when children watch others play. The onlooker may ask questions of other children, but there is no effort to join the play. This may happen when a child is shy, or unsure of the rules, or is hesitant to join the game.

<u>Age Range</u>: 2 years +

<u>Examples of Onlooker Play</u>: A child at a playground standing to the side watching the other kids use a seesaw, or a child watching two other kids build with blocks.

<u>How You Can Help</u>: Ask your child what they are noticing about the other kids playing. Gauge your child's interest in joining the play. If they do want to join the group, help them by giving them language they can use to join a game, or modeling how to do it by going over with them.

4. Parallel play – Parallel play starts when children begin to play side-by-side with other children without any interaction. Even though it seems like they are not interacting, they are paying attention to each other. This is the beginning of wanting to be with other children their age. This stage lays the groundwork for the later stages of play.

<u>Age Range</u>: 2 years +

<u>Examples of Parallel Play</u>: Building different sand castles side-by-side at the beach, or sitting beside each other on the floor, playing with completely different toys

<u>How You Can Help:</u> Ask your child what they notice about the other child's play. If they seem interested, suggest that they could both play together. For example, at the beach, you could suggest that they try to connect their two castles in some way.

5. Associative play – At some point, a child will start interacting more with the other child they are playing with; this is the next stage of play called associative play. They become more interested in other children than the toys. They start asking questions and talking about the toys and what they are making. This is the beginning of really understanding how to get along with others. During associative play, children within the group have similar goals. However, they do not set rules and there is no formal organization.

<u>Age Range:</u> 3 or 4 years +

<u>Examples of Associative Play:</u> building a creation out of blocks together, playing with cups together to make towers, playing with action figures together, racing cars

<u>How You Can Help:</u> This is where a lot of conflicts can arise, which is natural and expected. Often, there is a preferred race car that multiple children want to play with, or one of the children wants to knock over the towers before the others are done building. These conflicts are born out of learning. Kids haven't yet learned the rules of playing or interacting with

others, and this is how they test boundaries, and learn about group play.

Before you intervene, let them try to communicate with each other. See if they are able to come to a peaceable agreement. (Note: it's unlikely, especially early on, that this will work out, but trying is an important stage.)

If they aren't able to come up with a solution to their conflict, scaffold the play by helping them solve the problem together. Understand that this is the beginning of teachable moments for how to get along with others, to compromise, and to work together. It will be messy and it will not go well at first, because they are learning. Think of these times as teachable moments instead of bad behavior.

A Quick Note: When you hear "scaffold the play", think of scaffolding that goes up when a building is under construction. The scaffolding on the building is there as a support during the construction of the building. The same thing is true when we as parents are helping our children with play. When children are struggling on playdates, they will need extra support. You can scaffold their play by staying within earshot so you know what's happening. If things aren't getting resolved, then you can scaffold the play by stepping in and assisting them as they work through a conflict. If they need help figuring out what to play, you can scaffold by suggesting ideas.

The goal is to eventually have your child gain the skills to be on a playdate so that you can step back, and you don't have to be as involved anymore. It's like removing the scaffolding when the building is ready. When your child is ready, you can step back and they can figure out what to do on playdates, and resolve arguments on their own.

6. *Social play* – Children will begin to socialize more starting around three or four. They begin to share ideas and toys and follow established rules and guidelines. They play together and collaborate to determine who will play what role. They can work together to build something or maybe play a simple board game together. This is where a child learns and practices social skills, like cooperating, being flexible, taking turns, and solving problems.

Age Range: 3 or 4 years +

Examples of Social Play: playing a card game, working on a puzzle together, creating pretend play scenarios like playing shop, making food and serving it at a restaurant, playing house, creating a puppet show, running an animal hospital

How You Can Help: Social play leads to lots of teachable moments where kids are learning how to compromise, take turns, and be flexible. If they need help during social play, ask them which roles or jobs they need in their play, what materials they need, who will do what, etc.

Just as in associative play, it can get messy and there will be conflicts. These are those perfect teachable moments where we as the adults can help them through, and give them practice with these important social skills.

SOCIAL STAGES OF PLAY

Unoccupied Play

The random movements that Infants make with no clear purpose is the beginning of play.

Solitary Play

When children start to play on their own. Children do not seem to notice other children sitting or playing nearby during this type of play

Onlooker Play

When children watch others play. The child who is looking may ask questions but there is no effort to join the play.

Parallel Play

When children begins to play side-by-side with other children without any interaction. They are paying attention to each other.

Associative Play

When children start asking questions of each other. They have similar goals but there are no set rules.

Social Play

When children begin to share ideas and toys, and follow established rules and guidelines.

How Play Helps

It can be hard to watch as kids struggle with play and social skill development. We want to support them and teach them socially acceptable ways of interacting. So, we talk to them, maybe do a few worksheets, and talk about expected behaviors. And sometimes, they can tell us exactly what the expectations are in those isolated moments. However, when they are faced with the same situation in real life, it doesn't translate. How do we teach kids social skills so that kids will use them in other areas of life? **The best way to teach social skills is to use play.**

Dr. Stuart Brown has done extensive research on play. He says that when people use play to learn, the lessons "seem to be fixed more strongly and last longer" than through other methods of learning. Let's use the power of play to help our children learn and retain skills.

I saw this especially when teaching social skills groups. The best model I found was teaching the skill, then setting up a real-life practice of the skill with adult support. We would talk about a particular skill, then actually use that skill while we were playing in a group setting. For instance, we may talk about the skill of listening, then play a game of Uno, and practice our listening skills. When kids were doing a good job listening, the adults would give positive feedback. If kids were having challenges listening, then the adult would be able to step in and give reminders of what good listening looks like. Adults could even model it.

For families, the playdate is a real-life situation where kids can practice interactions with others. On a playdate, if your child is struggling, then you can be a support for them just like the adults in a social skills group I described. You can review what the expectations are before the playdate starts. When things are going well, you can give them that positive feedback. If they need help to get things back on track, you can step in and do that. In the next chapter, there are more details about how to set up a playdate to make it as successful as possible.

CHAPTER 1: PLAYDATES AND SOCIAL SKILLS

Playdates are a great way for kids to interact and spend time together. Playdates are typically scheduled ahead of time, and involve fun activities, enjoying one another's company, and strengthening their friendship bond. Some kids can figure out what they're going to do without any issues; they cooperate and get along for the most part, and everyone leaves the playdate in good space.

But what about those kids who struggle during playdates? For these kids, the things that can be challenging in day-to-day life (i.e. following directions, sharing, taking turns, working together, cooperating) are magnified in an unstructured social situation like a free-for-all playdate.

Rick Lavoie, author of It's So Much Work to be Your Friend, talks about the spiral of social skills to help kids who struggle to develop these important parts of themselves. First, you learn the skills, then apply and use them in real social situations. Those positive interactions make it more likely that your circle of friends will grow, allowing for more social opportunities, and more chances to practice those skills.
In order to get better at these skills, you need to use them in real situations.

When we host a playdate or our child attends a playdate, this is that real life situation. **A playdate creates a teachable moment where our children can practice and grow their social skills.**

How to Set the Stage for a Successful Playdate

Playdates for kids who struggle socially, when done thoughtfully, offer an opportunity for kids to practice social skills and have a positive interaction with another child. We can set our kids up for success on playdates while they continue to hone their skills. Here are some ideas to help you set the stage for a successful playdate.

Start small
If your child is struggling socially, keep playdates to just a single friend. When you add in another child or two, that adds to the complexity of the interactions and social skills needed to compromise, take turns, and work together. The goal is to have them experience some success, and starting small is a great foundation. If things go well, you can always add in more children in the future.

Start at your home
If you think your child may have difficulty on a playdate, it may work best to have a first playdate with a friend at your own house. Your child may feel more comfortable in a familiar

environment. You'll be able to keep an eye and ear out during the playdate so you can step in if things start to break down.

Prepare your child ahead of time

Preparing for a playdate might seem simple, but if you provide multiple opportunities for your child to get used to the idea, it will increase their control of the situation, and help them to feel more comfortable from the outset.

Some things you can do to prepare your child include:

1. **Let your child choose his or her playmate.** Talk with your child about who they want to invite over to the house. Help them choose one child who seems friendly and kind. This way, they're already involved in the planning of the event.

2. **Go over the rules.** Remind your child to be polite and respectful to your guests. Talk through specifics, like "How can you show respect during a board game?" or "How can you be polite even if you don't agree with your friend?" or "What happens if your friend wants to play a game and you don't want to?" If your child has special items or toys that they don't want others to play with, move them to a safe spot where they won't be touched.

3. **Set a clear time frame, and keep it short.** Schedule a playdate for only an hour or two. An open-ended playdate can be overwhelming. Limiting the time will make it more

likely that the experience is positive and ends on a good note. Keep the time frame in mind as you think about which activities you'll do. It would be a challenge to complete a game of Monopoly in an hour, but you could definitely play several rounds of Connect 4.

4. **Stay close by and keep an ear out.** You don't need to be in the same room with them the whole time, but you also need to be ready to step in if you need to. You know when it's getting to be too much for your child. If things start to get too feisty or they're not interacting well, be prepared to move in.

5. **Feed them.** Kids love yummy snacks, and snack time can be a transitional activity if things start to get bumpy. You can even make a snack together as an activity. Don't forget to check in regarding allergies and other dietary restrictions before serving anything.

6. **Provide gentle guidance, if needed.** Sometimes kids don't know what to do, or what to play. To avoid potential conflicts (or demands for a screen-based activity), it can be helpful to step in and give them some ideas. Plus, if kids are struggling with figuring out what to do, simply by suggesting an activity you've given them something to talk about. It gives them a place to begin if they are stuck and overwhelmed.

7. **Use this book.** There are 50 ideas you can set up without too much fuss to give them a starting point for play. They may not end up playing that same game or activity that you suggest. That's OK! The whole point was to inspire them to play. Even if it's not playing in the way that you expected them to play, they're still doing something playful.

How to Set up a Play-friendly Home

1. **Eliminate what they don't use.** Get rid of toys that your children no longer play with or have outgrown. You can give them new homes by having a yard sale, donating them, or giving them away to younger family and friends. If a toy is broken beyond repair, find a way to recycle it, or just throw it away. You can repurpose some parts of broken toys and games. For instance, if a puzzle is missing a ton of pieces, you could use that as part of a tinker tray for creation. Studies have shown that having fewer toys increases a child's ability to be creative and imaginative with the toys they do have and use - less is more!

2. **Organize what you have.** Make a plan for toys -- what will stay in a child's room, a playroom, living room, or another shared space? You can even designate certain areas for certain types of toys. Perhaps you'll have one or two drawers dedicated to arts and crafts, a place where

you put your coloring books and drawing paper, a shelf where board and card games go, and a space for LEGOs®.

3. **Create a Toy Rotation Plan.** Children love novelty. How can you create novelty without buying new things all the time? Use a toy rotation. Keep some toys in a closet, garage, or basement, then periodically switch out what is available. Suddenly, the marble maze they haven't played with in months feels brand new again, and keeps them busy for a longer time. This also gives an opportunity to figure out what they still love, what they don't like anymore, and allows for additional weeding out of toys that are no longer of interest.

4. **Get versatile and/or high interest toys.** Focus on getting open-ended toys because of their versatility. Open-ended toys are ones that can be used in multiple ways. The more ways a toy can be used, the better for encouraging creativity and imagination. Plus having toys that can be used in multiple ways cuts down on having to find storage for all of them.

   Some examples of open ended toys include K'Nex®, Connectagons®, LEGOs and DUPLOs®, Magna-Tiles®, wooden blocks, dolls/stuffed animals, or play dough. A cash register, pretend money, and dress up items can be awesome supports for pretend play, socio-dramatic play, and imaginative scenes. Try to avoid toys that can only be played with in one way. For more information and ideas about open ended toys, see Chapter 6.

5. **Remember that collections can be cool.** Sometimes children find a type of toy that they have a real deep interest and passion for – that's developmentally expected and appropriate. My own children went through a stage of loving Shopkins™ and Stikbots®. Pay attention to what your child is drawn to, and talk about it. Keep the lines of communication open around whether or not they want to continue to grow their collection. I'd never tell a child to get rid of their beloved Pokemon card collection, but there may come a time where they do outgrow certain collections. While we still love Stikbots at our home, the Shopkins have been passed on to another family.

6. **Keep track of arts and crafts supplies.** Keep track of what you have will allow you to know what you are low on, and then you can stock up. When you know your kids will be home for an extended vacation or for summer, take a few moments to inventory what you have, and stock up so you're ready to play. The worksheet on the next page can help you figure out what you do and don't have to help get yourself prepared.

Play Supplies

Arts & Crafts

- ☐ Paper (different colors and weights)
- ☐ Scissors
- ☐ Tape (washi, duct tape, or scotch tape)
- ☐ Watercolor paint
- ☐ Crayons/Colored Pencils/Markers
- ☐ Sidewalk chalk
- ☐ Felt, Thread & Needles
- ☐ Pipe cleaners
- ☐ Fabric
- ☐ Yarn
- ☐ Origami Paper
- ☐ Glue or Mod Podge®
- ☐ Salt
- ☐ Q-Tips
- ☐ Paper Cups
- ☐ Sequins

Games/Activities

- ☐ Sunprints®
- ☐ Magic Nuudles®
- ☐ Water Beads
- ☐ 2 player board games
- ☐ 2 player card games
- ☐ Peaceable Kingdom® games
- ☐ Mad Libs™
- ☐ Tent/Fort Making Supplies
- ☐ Story Cubes®
- ☐ Bowling Set
- ☐ Hand Trampoline
- ☐ Jump Rope
- ☐ Stomp Rockets
- ☐ Frisbees
- ☐ Gym mat
- ☐ Puzzles

Pretend Play Materials

- ☐ Pretend Food
- ☐ Dishes, flatware and cups
- ☐ Cash Register
- ☐ Wands
- ☐ Capes & Masks
- ☐ Dress up Clothes & Jewelry
- ☐ Hats
- ☐ Eye patches
- ☐ Envelopes
- ☐ Paper bags
- ☐ Boxes of food containers from recycling
- ☐ Doctor's kit
- ☐ Stuffed Animals
- ☐ Toy cars & trucks
- ☐ Action Figures
- ☐ Baby Blankets and shoeboxes

Open Ended Play Supplies

- ☐ Sand (kinetic or playground sand)
- ☐ Sand Tray
- ☐ Tray with several separate compartments
- ☐ Water table
- ☐ Small figures
- ☐ Natural materials like stones, shells, flowers, sticks, leaves, seeds, etc.
- ☐ Containers and scoops of different sizes
- ☐ Materials from the recycling bin
- ☐ Foil, tissue paper, ribbon
- ☐ Cardboard boxes & tubes
- ☐ Baking soda & Vinegar for experiments
- ☐ Flour & Oil for Cloud Dough
- ☐ Water & Cornstarch for Oobleck
- ☐ Glue, Baking Soda & contact lens solution for slime

Keeping Crafts

There are going to be a lot of activities in this book, especially this section, where kids can create something. However, it's impossible to keep everything that your child makes forever. Here are some ideas to help you manage the arts and crafts creations:

1. Have a chat with your child and explain that it is impossible to keep everything forever, because your home would be too full! Explain that there will be a few things that you keep forever, but there will be some things you keep for just a little bit, and then recycle, donate, pass on to someone else, or throw away.

2. Create an arts and crafts display area in your home to show off some of their favorites, and then change out the creations for new ones. You can do the switching, but it can also be helpful to eventually involve your child to help pick which items to display and which items should move on.

3. To make the most of the things you are only keeping for a little bit, you can take pictures of the creations they've made so they have a memory of it. You could post a picture on Instagram, or make a photo book of some of their artwork to keep for later.

Initially, it may be less painful to wait until the child is not present to get rid of some of their projects. And to be honest, I have done that myself. But over time, start to let your child get more involved with the decision making. Let the child get practice with picking what they want to keep and saying goodbye to things they don't.

CHAPTER 2: CREATIVE PLAY

Sir Ken Robinson is an education and creativity expert, and has spoken all over the world. He recorded one of the most watched TED talks, all about creativity and schools, and he identifies creativity as an essential skill for children. He said that "creativity is as important now in education as literacy and we should treat it with the same status."

The following activities encourage creativity in our children by allowing them to explore, try out new ideas and use their imagination. They can use lots of different items, altering one or two things, and making something new. When doing these activities with another person, children will get a chance to problem solve, communicate, and listen to one another. They will also make mistakes, and learn how to manage those, plus they will get opportunities to deal with frustration in a healthy way.

One of my favorite ways to encourage creativity is to use arts and crafts. There are several arts-and-crafts-based activities below to help kids to hone their imagination skills and create whatever comes to mind. This helps kids practice flexible and innovative thinking.

Make a Paper Cup Tower

Age range: 3 +
Mess level: 1 out of 3
Indoor or outdoor: Indoor

Skill Highlight: Building towers helps kids practice *patience*. They may make some mistakes as they go along, and if they want to build a higher tower, they'll need to keep persevering.

Materials needed:
- Small white paper cups
- An even surface to stack them up

Directions:
Paper cups are one of the least expensive and most versatile toys. Children can build towers of all different shapes and sizes, and then knock them down in different ways, like using catapults, or paper planes, or ping pong balls, or toy cars. Children can work together on a large tower, or build their own individual towers.

Here are some examples of different towers children can build!

Have Fun with Water Beads

This is a creative activity that can also be a calming sensory activity. Water beads arrive really small, so to get the water beads more ready to play with, you can put them in water before the playdate. This process can take hours though, so if you're having a short playdate, it may make more sense to put them in water a few hours before the playdate begins. Another option is to add water to the beads and let the kids watch as they get bigger and absorb the water, then add more water and see how big they will get.

Age range: 3 +
Mess level: 2 out of 3

Indoor or outdoor: Either!

Skills Highlight: When kids are working with water beads together, this can help them practice *working together*. If they are working in one container, they will have to figure out how to play in the space together. This also helps them work on *understanding personal space*, and figure out their comfort level while playing in the same space as others - how close feels too close? What if your hands touch? What if your friend goes into your space when playing with the beads? If it becomes too much to handle, you as the adult can separate the beads into two different containers and have them play side by side.

Materials:
- Water beads
- Water
- Container in which to play with beads

Directions:
You can keep it very simple and just set out the water beads and have kids place their hands in and play with the water beads. Or you can add in water safe items into the tub for sensory play. You can also use measuring cups and spoons and different size containers to pour the beads into and out of for fun. You can add in other materials, like shaving cream or slime or different types of water.

Build Tents and Forts

Do you remember making forts when you were little? Encourage your kids to do the same. They can use materials in your home or there are several fort making kits available on the market for kids. Allow them to be creative and build forts together.

You can also put out a tent as part of a play date. They can bring other things inside, create a pretend campground, make a little house for dolls or figures, etc.

Age range: 3 +

Mess level: 2 out of 3
Indoor or outdoor: Indoor

Skills Highlight: This is all about *thinking flexibly*. Kids can look at the materials around them and figure out different ways to use these other materials. If their fort falls apart, then they have to *problem solve* to make it stand up or work in a different way. Forts & tents also foster independence, since allow kids to create their own elaborate spaces.

Materials:
Couch cushions, dining tables and chairs, cardboard boxes, blankets or sheets can make some pretty elaborate forts or tents.

Directions:
Encourage the kids to think about creating forts and tents in a unique way using what is available. Yes, you can sit at a dining room table in a chair. But you can also put a sheet over the table and make a fort. Or turn the chairs a different way to make a tunnel. Tents can be used in a variety of ways. A tent can be a campground, or a doll hospital or a cave.

Play in Sand Trays

This is such a relaxing sensory activity for kids to do. It allows for a lot of creative and imaginative thinking. They may start to play out scenes or add in other things to play with, or just enjoy running their fingers through the sand, hiding and digging up items.

Age range: 3 +
Mess level: 3 out of 3
Indoor or outdoor: Outdoor

Skills Highlight: This activity is perfect for *flexible thinking*. What can we do with these materials? What other things can we play with? What happens if we add in different toys?

Materials:

- A container with sand or kinetic sand
- Small figures (Toobs® available at Michael's or Amazon work really well)
- Small rocks, stones and/or shells
- Scoop/spoon/small shovel
- Other small items

Directions:

Set out materials in an open space where the kids can move around easily, and watch what happens. Consider planning around a theme, like dinosaurs or space or robots.

Draw Pictures

This can be a great creative quiet activity for kids to do on a playdate together. They can work side by side making their own pictures, while they work on sharing the arts materials in front of them. Plus you can just use what you have in your home right now, no special trips to the store required!

Age range: 3 +
Mess level: 2 out of 3
Indoor or outdoor: Indoor

Skills Highlight: Seeing how another person uses the same materials you have but in a different way is a neat way to work on *understanding someone else's point of view*. Different kids will create very different pictures using the same materials.

Materials:
- Paper – construction, cardboard, white paper, etc. – whatever you have available
- Drawing Materials – colored pencils, markers, crayons, paints, etc.

Directions:

This is a great open-ended play opportunity. Set the kids up with art materials and a safe, even surface to work on. Kids can draw whatever they like using what's in front of them. If you want you can also include glue, tape and scissors to allow for even more ways to create.

Use Some Sidewalk Chalk

Sidewalk chalk is a great way to encourage movement, creativity, and collaboration. With sidewalk chalk, kids can create a hopscotch game, they can mark a start and finish line for races, or if they're feeling super inspired, they can make their own gigantic board game. Or, they can simply draw pictures and write words, pour water over it and see what happens. So much fun!

Age range: 3 +
Mess level: 2 out of 3
Indoor or outdoor: Outdoor

<u>Skills Highlight</u>: This is a cool way for kids to *work together*. They may have two very different ideas for how to use the sidewalk chalk. They'll need to *communicate* with one another, listen to the other person and work together!

Materials:
- Sidewalk chalk
- A place to draw

Directions:
Not much to direct here! Give them some chalk and see what they create.

Play with Magic Nuudles®

Magic Nuudles are a great material that only requires one additional thing to use – water! They are biodegradable, and you don't need any glue to make them stick, just simple water. They stick to paper and one another so this is an excellent material to use to make all kinds of creations including 3D sculptures. Kids can get as creative as they want.

Age range: 3 +
Mess level: 2 out of 3
Indoor or outdoor: Either one!

<u>Skills Highlight</u>: This is a great activity to help kids *understand another person's perspective.* Two kids may play use the Nuudles and create vastly different items.

Materials:
- Magic Nuudles
- Water

Directions:
Put out these items along with a little water and watch the kids use their imaginations.

Be Creative with Sun Prints®

This is a great activity to do on a sunny day. There is a neat and unexpected reaction that occurs when you put items on sunprint paper in the sun for just a few minutes. After those few minutes, then you see the shadow of the items on the sunprint. There are small sun prints and larger ones as well, so kids can try multiple shapes and materials.

Age range: 3 +

Mess level: 2 out of 3

Indoor or outdoor: Outdoor

<u>Skills Highlight</u>: This activity encourages *creativity* and *innovation*. Children can use different materials to create different shadows on the sun prints. After they see their first batch, they may want to try varying the materials they used, putting them in a different way to create a different shadow. Maybe they can even integrate their sunprints into a bigger art activity.

Materials:
- Sun Prints
- Materials like sticks, rocks, blocks, figures, etc to place on top of the sunprint paper

Directions:
Explain what will happen when the prints are laid out in the sun. Help the kids collect items that they want to place on top of the paper, and then place the prints out to see what happens!

Create Art Using Nature

Using natural materials is a fun way to introduce new textures and different ways to create art.

Age range: 3 +
Mess level: 2 out of 3
Indoor or outdoor: Either!

Skills Highlight: This is another activity that can help kids *understand someone else's point of view*. Although they'll be using the same materials, their art will probably look very different. Even on different days, using the same materials, the artwork produced may be very different.

Materials:

- Leaves, small sticks, small stones, and other materials gathered from outdoors

- Arts and crafts materials – paper, popsicle sticks, googly eyes, yarn, pom poms, markers, crayons, etc.

Directions:

Talk to the kids about possible ways to use the materials, and let them decide what sounds like fun. For instance, they can do something as simple as leaf rubbing. They can start by gathering leaves, putting the leaves between two pieces of paper, and using the side of a crayon to rub the impression of the leaf onto the top piece of paper.

They may also decide to use natural materials to create art. They can glue leaves onto paper, and add in other arts and crafts materials to make characters or creatures. They can make 3D art using pinecones and other crafting materials.

Build a Fairy Garden

Creating a fairy garden is a great way to have kids *work together* and use creative thinking. Fairy gardens combine imaginative and creative arts play. This is one of the more whimsical of our activities!

Age range: 3 +
Mess level: 2 out of 3
Indoor or outdoor: Either!

Skills Highlight: This is another activity that works on *thinking flexibly*. What can popsicle sticks make that would work in a fairy garden? How can we use stones? What size materials will work for fairies to use? Making a garden like this encourages kids to *be creative* as they think of different ways to use everyday items.

Suggested Materials:
- Container/space outdoors for the garden
- Small figures
- Beads
- Stones
- Small low growing plants/moss
- Popsicle Sticks
- Toothpicks

Directions:

There are so many different ways you can create a fairy garden. You can start with a spot in your yard, or you can create one inside in a pot or a small plastic bin. You could purchase some items to start creating a garden, but it's also fun to make items for one. You can plan out what you will do, or just wing it.

The only important thing is to allow the kids to use their creativity as they build, and encourage them to be flexible about what they want to use.

Put on a Puppet Show

Creating a puppet show is a fun way for kids to pass the time, while being creative about the topic of the play, the characters in the play, and the story line.

Age range: 3 +
Mess level: 1 out of 3
Indoor or outdoor: Indoor

Skills Highlight: This type of activity involves *listening* to your friend as you create a puppet show, and come up with different ideas for what kind of show to make, what characters should be involved, who should say what, etc. If there's not a script for the play, you have to listen to what others are saying to have a story that makes sense.

Suggested Materials:
- Cardboard box/shoebox
- Characters for the play
- Ideas for a plot
- Dialogue for the play

Directions:

Plan out some possible themes ahead of time, but let the kids take the lead as much as possible. Make suggestions for puppet characters they can create. Even the puppet show stage can be created and decorated. Kids can use a cardboard box or a shoe box to create a place to hold the show. Or maybe use items around the house in different ways to create a stage.

Paint with Q-Tips

This is a way to paint using a different type of material that keeps the paint a little neater, but allows for different ways of painting. This allows for so much *creativity*! They can use small dots to create patterns and images, or see what happens when they use the q-tips more like a paintbrush.

Age range: 3 +
Mess level: 3 out of 3
Indoor or outdoor: Either!

Skills Highlight: This is the perfect opportunity to practice *thinking outside the box*. Usually you use paintbrushes to paint. But by using other materials you can create different sorts of patterns and shapes.

Materials:

- Paint in separate containers
- Q-Tips
- Paper

Directions:

Set out the paper, paint and q-tips, and see what they create! You can even give them additional different materials to paint with, like a colander or pinecones or sponges. What sorts of different ideas does that help kids make?

Paint Rocks

It may sound like a simple activity, but painting rocks gives kids a chance to decorate something three-dimensional and tangible.

Age range: 3 +
Mess level: 3 out of 3
Indoor or outdoor: Either!

Skills Highlight: This is an activity that encourages *creativity* and can also be an opportunity to practice kindness and thinking of others. Children can paint the rocks, and give them to one another, or use them as a way to practice a random act of kindness by placing them around in the neighborhood, park, playground, or walking path in the neighborhood.

Materials:
- Smooth rocks
- Paint/permanent markers
- Mod Podge® (glue/sealer that you can purchase at stores like Michael's or Hobby Lobby)

Directions:

Have kids design and paint the rocks in whatever way they'd like. Once the painting is dry, they can cover the rocks with Mod Podge as a sealer to make it last longer. You can have kids exchange the rocks they made with each other, or save them for future kind acts.

Paint with Salt

This is a cool way to do a painting project.

Age range: 3 +
<u>Mess level</u>: 3 out of 3
Indoor or outdoor: Either!

<u>Skills Highlight</u>: This helps kids work on *dealing with mistakes.* Some paint may drip in an area that you weren't expecting. Or the paint flows differently than from what you anticipated. It's not going to be perfect, and that's ok!

Materials:
- Glue
- Table salt
- Watercolors
- Droppers/paintbrushes
- Sturdy paper, cardstock, or cardboard

Paint with Salt

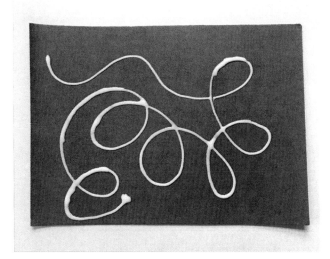

Create a pattern on heavy
paper or cardstock using glue.

②

Sprinkle the salt onto it.

③

Shake off the excess salt and
let it dry

④

Using paintbrushes or droppers,
dab a little bit of paint onto
the different parts of the
design. As you dab the paint
on, it will spread through the
salt crystals.

5

Keep going until every part
has a color, then let it dry.
Enjoy your beautiful
creation!

If you want, you can make several glue & salt creations
before your playdate buddy comes over. That way, they
will be dry and ready for painting. Once you've painted
the creations, your friend can take home their creations
and let them dry at home.

Create Your Own Paper Airplanes

Age range: 5 +

<u>Mess level</u>: 1 out of 3

Indoor or outdoor: Either!

<u>Skill Highlight</u>: This is a great activity to help kids practice *following directions*. It's fun to make paper airplanes, but if you want to have a plan that flies well, or you want to try a new type of plane, kids will need to follow directions in order to do that.

Materials needed:
- White 8.5 x 11 paper
- Crayons/Markers/Colored Pencils
- Target or Finish Line

Make a Paper Airplane

1

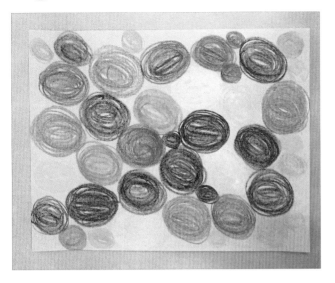

Decorate your piece of paper any way you'd like – you can use patterns, blocks of colors, shapes, etc. Once you're done, then you turn it into an airplane.

2

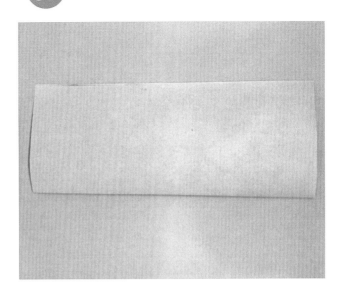

Take that piece of paper and fold it in half lengthwise.

3

Open it up again and bring the corners down to meet the crease in the middle (it makes two triangles).

4

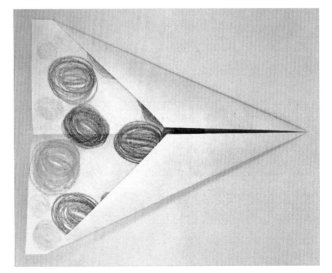

Take the corners of the small triangles and fold those in again to meet the crease in the middle

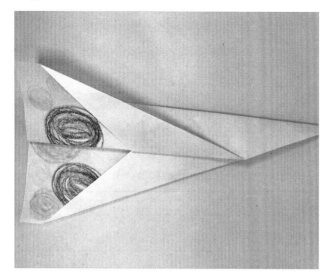

Now it's time to make the wings. Put the airplane on it's side and fold one half down part way to make a wing. Repeat with the other side.

Lift up the wings and your plane is ready to fly!

Once your planes are done, of course you have to test them. See how far everyone's planes go. Place the target a little distance away or a line on the ground to see if you can reach it.

Write a Comic Book

Graphic novels are a type of book that is growing in popularity. There are some popular books out there that use comics within the text, like <u>Big Nate</u>, <u>Captain Underpants</u>, and <u>Diary of a Wimpy Kid</u>. Kids can use these as a jumping off point to make their own comics. They can keep it simple and just make one page, or they can start to make a whole series of different comics.

Age range: 5 +
<u>Mess level</u>: 1 out of 3
Indoor or outdoor: Indoor

Skills Highlight: To make a comic book, you have to *work together.* Who will do the drawing and the writing? Will you both share those responsibilities? How do you incorporate different ideas? Writing a comic book can help kids practice thinking about how others might react in certain situations, and *taking someone else's perspective* in different scenarios.

Materials:
- Blank comic book pages (included here)
- Or make your own and draw on thought and talk bubbles
- Or use thought or talk bubble stickers

Directions:
Let kids get their creative juices flowing. If they get stuck, suggest a few scenarios for them. Ask them questions like: what kind of character do you want to create? What should your character do? How does this person feel right now? What's the best way to end this story?

Weave with Paper

The repetitive rhythmic nature of weaving can be soothing and relaxing for kids. Plus when they're sitting and doing it together, they can start to chat and practice conversation skills.

They learn to follow a simple pattern, and manage frustration when things don't go quite as expected. Plus they can create something they can use as a decoration.

Age range: 5 +
Mess level: 1 out of 3
Indoor or outdoor: Indoor

<u>Skills Highlight</u>: This may be an activity that offers a chance to practice *managing frustration*. It may not work the way kids want the first time, so encourage them to persevere and handle not getting it right the first time in a safe and healthy way.

Materials Needed:
- Paper in different colors, 8.5" x 11"
- Scissors
- Glue

Other materials kids can use to weave:
- Cardboard rectangles and yarn
- Paper plates with notches all around and yarn
- Branches

Weave with Paper

1

Fold a piece of
paper in half so the
short sides line up.

2

Cut evenly-spaced slits
starting from the folded edge
and stopping about 1 inch from
the opposite edge. (You can
draw vertical lines as a guide,
which would help younger kids)

3

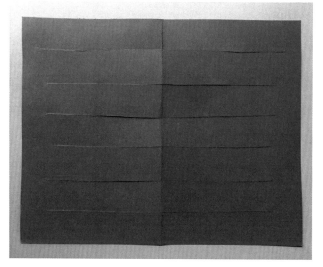

Unfold the paper.

4

Cut paper strips from
different colored paper.

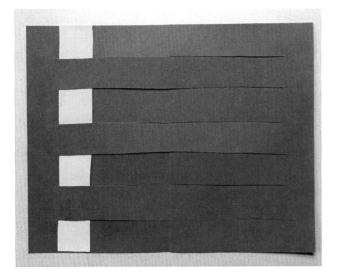

Take one paper strip and weave it by going over and under the slits one by one.

Weave the second strip in an opposite way as the first strip. For example, If your first strip went over and under the slits, the second strip should go under and over the slits.

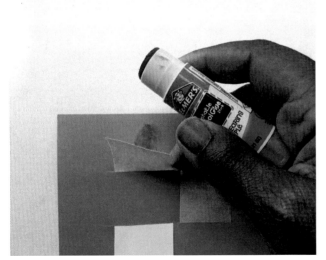

Once the strips are in place, glue them so they don't move.

Continue until the whole paper is full.

Create and Decode Secret Messages

It's fun to have a secret! Kids love to share secret messages, and there are so many ways to create secret messages for kids to find. This is a quick & simple way for kids to share secret messages with one another.

Age range: 8 +

Mess level: 2 out of 3

Indoor or outdoor: Indoor or outdoor

Skill Highlight: This activity is all about *communication*. There are lots of different ways to communicate, and sometimes it's easier to pick up on those hints. Other times, an idea may be more hidden. This is a great way to help kids practice a different form of communicating with one another.

Materials:
- White crayons
- Strips of white paper
- Watercolors
- Water

Directions:

Have each child write a secret message to the other, using the white crayons on the white paper. Then have the kids exchange papers. Use the watercolors to paint over the paper. When the kids paint over the message, the words will be revealed!

Sew with Felt

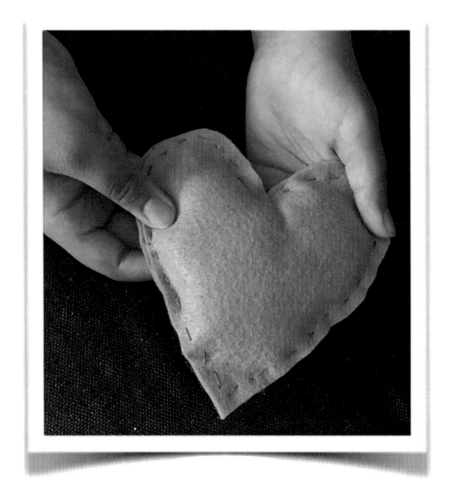

Felt sewing is a more challenging activity, but it's also one that allows for so much creativity and imagination.

Age range: 8 +
Mess level: 2 out of 3
Indoor or outdoor: Indoor

Skills Highlight: This is the perfect opportunity to practice *patience.* It can take a little time to design, cut out the felt, sew it together, stuff it and finish the project.

Materials:
- Cardboard
- Felt
- String / yarn
- Needle
- Scissors
- Stuffing/Polyfill/Cotton balls

Here are some simple ideas for things to create:
- Pillows – all you need is two rectangles or squares
- Pincushion
- Simple stuffed animal
- Simple shapes – heart or diamond or rectangle, etc.

Sew with Felt

 1

Help the kids figure out what they want to make, then draw it on a piece of cardboard and cut it out.

 2

Using the cardboard as a template, trace the pattern onto two pieces of felt, then cut the felt shapes out.

3

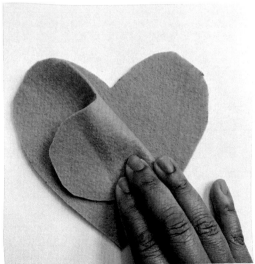

Stack the two pieces of felt one on top of another.

4

Take a piece of thread, and put it in the eye of a needle. Make a knot at the end of the string.

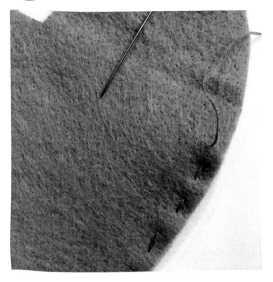

Using a simple running stitch (going up and down through both pieces of felt) sew the two pieces of felt together.

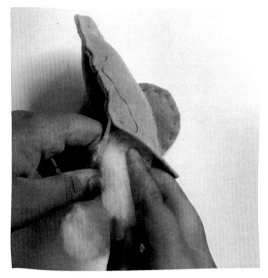

When you get about 3/4 of the way around, stop and stuff your creation with polyfill/cotton batting/cotton balls to make it soft and give it 3D structure.

Once it is stuffed, finish by going the rest of the way around your creation and tying a knot

Enjoy your new creation!

Knit with Your Fingers

This is a good introduction to using yarn for creativity. Finger knitting can be done using two, three, or four fingers.

Age range: 8 +
Mess level: 1 out of 3
Indoor or outdoor: Indoor

<u>Skills Highlight</u>: This is another activity that can help kids *think flexibly.* Once kids created a length of finger knitting, then creativity can take over. What can you do with this string of finger knitted yarn. Make a scarf? A small cuddly doll? A ball? A rug? Decorations for a room? There are so many possibilities! Plus, if kids like this activity, they may enjoy knitting on a loom, or learning to knit using needles.

Materials:
  • Ball of yarn (wool, cotton, or acrylic)

Note: If you need to interrupt your finger knitting, you can put the loops on a fork or on straws rubber banded together.

An alternative idea – Have the kids use a knitting loom. This also makes it much easier to take a break from the project since they yarn will be on the loom, not their fingers.

Knit with your Fingers

To begin, take the end of a piece of yarn and hold it in place using your thumb.

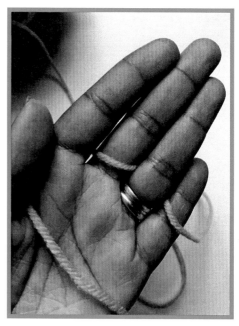

Weave yarn back and forth around your fingers...

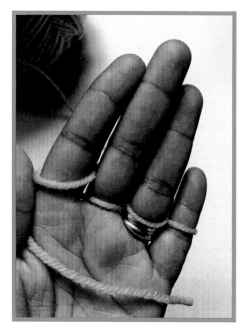

until each finger you are using has yarn on both sides. This is your base row.

Weave back and forth again...

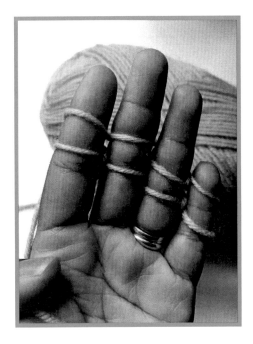

until you have two rows on your fingers.

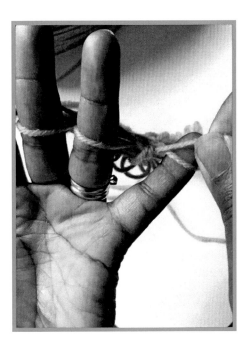

Take the bottom row, and loop it off your fingers, leaving the top row on. You should have one row left on your fingers.

Weave yarn back and forth again

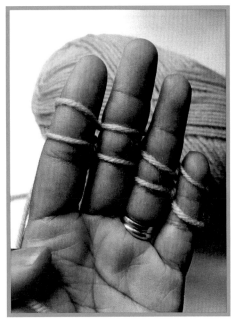

until there are two complete rows on your finger again.

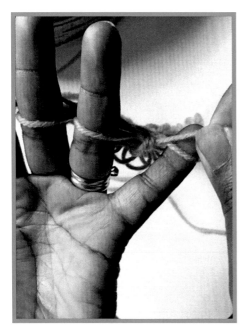

Take the bottom row, and loop it off your fingers, leaving the top row on. You should have one row left on your fingers.

As you continue to add a row and loop off the bottom row, you will start to get a trail of woven yarn over the back of your hand.

When you get to a length you want, leave one row on your fingers. Leave several inches, and cut it off from the rest of the ball of yarn.

Take the end of the yarn you just cut off, and loop it through the first loop on your finger.

Continue to pull the string through all four loops on your fingers.

Pull it off of your fingers...

make a knot and tighten.

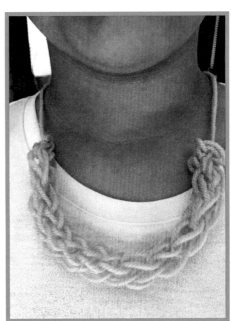

What will you make with your finger knitting? A bracelet, a necklace, a scarf, a small ball, decorations for a room? Get creative!

Make Your Own Secret Code

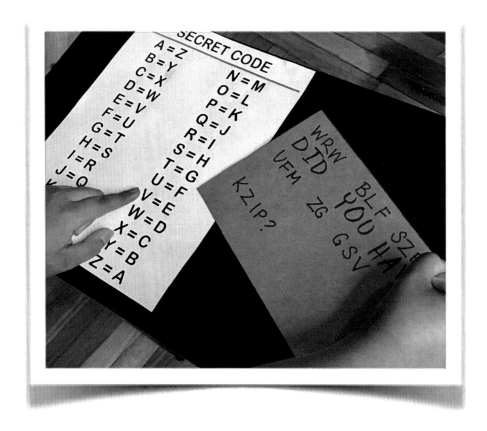

This is another activity all about practicing communication. Kids can start with the secret code provided, and then once they get the hang of it, they can make up their own.

Age range: 8 +

Mess level: 1 out of 3

Indoor or outdoor: Indoor or outdoor

Skill Highlight: This activity is not only about *communicating*, but *working together* to solve a problem. How can you figure out what the message is? What if you are having a hard time? How can you solve that problem?

Materials:
- Secret code (prepare this in advance)
- Pencils or markers or something else to write with

Directions:
Have kids use secret code on the next page and come up with a simple sentence to translate. Have each child write their sentence in code. Once they're done, have children exchange their codes and translate them. Using the secret code provided, they can practice writing messages to decode to one another. Then, if they want to keep going, they can write more sentences.

Next level challenge: Kids can be innovative and make up their own secret code.

SECRET CODE

A = Z	N = M
B = Y	O = L
C = X	P = K
D = W	Q = J
E = V	R = I
F = U	S = H
G = T	T = G
H = S	U = F
I = R	V = E
J = Q	W = D
K = P	X = C
L = O	Y = B
M = N	Z = A

Craft with Duct Tape

Duct tape has become some popular over the last several years. There are lots of projects involving duct tape, and so many varieties of duct tape available now that you can create tons of different items. Some people have even created entire prom dresses using duct tape! Your kids don't have to get that intricate – they can start with easy things like a duct tape wallet, with or without a flap.

Age range: 8 +
Mess level: 2 out of 3
Indoor or outdoor: Indoor

Skill Highlight: Duct tape crafts can be fun, but also challenging. This is another activity that helps kids practice that ever important skill of *managing frustrations*. How will you react when the duct tape sticks to you? Or won't stick where you want?

Materials for Simple Wallet:
• One or two rolls of duct tape

Materials for Wallet with Flap:
• Two different patterns of duct tape
• Velcro squares or circles

Simple Duct Tape Wallet

1

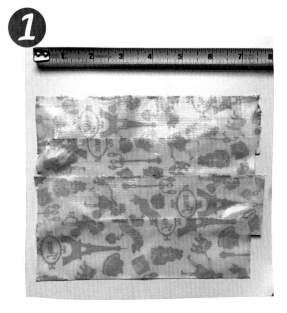

Take 4 strips of tape about 7" long, lay them next to each other, slightly overlapping

2

Lay 4 other trips of duct tape about 7" long on top of the first 4 strips, sticky sides facing each other. You should have a big rectangle of duct tape.

3

4

Trim the sides of the rectangle so they are even, and big enough for a dollar bill.

5

Fold rectangle in half the long way, and take two 3" pieces of duct tape and place on each side.

6

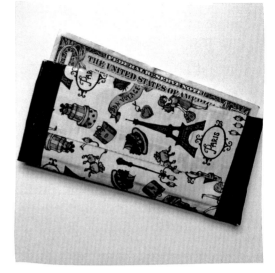

Push the tape to the back. The wallet is done!

Duct Tape Wallet with Flap

1

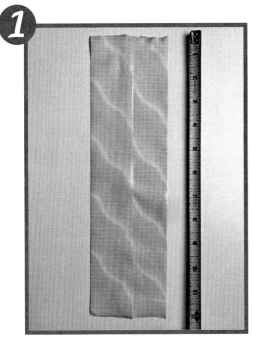

Take 2 strips of duct tape about 12 inches long and lay out the long way, slightly overlapping.

2

Then layer on two other long strips of duct tape.

3

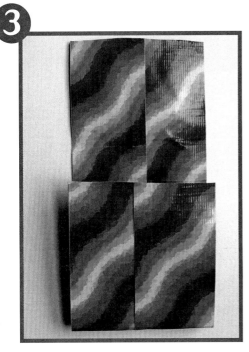

Fold long duct tape rectangle into thirds.

4

Cut a triangle on one end.

5

Tape up the two sides,
leaving the triangle flap
open.

6

Place velcro on the
triangle tab, and put the
corresponding velcro
material on the other side.

Fold Your Own Origami

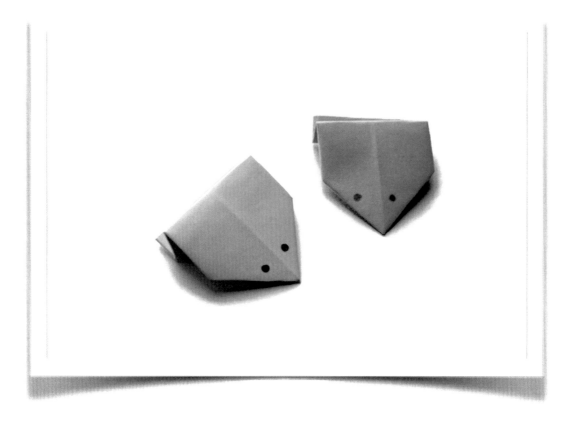

Doing a simple origami activity can be fun. The origami they make can then be used in different ways to play. They could set up a store (pretend or real) and sell origami. They can use their origami in a scene they create with blocks, **LEGO**® bricks or cardboard. They can attach their origami to popsicle sticks and create a puppet show.

Age range: 8 **+**
Mess level: 1 out of 3
Indoor or outdoor: Indoor

Skill Highlight: Origami helps kids with concentration and *patience*. It's a quiet activity, but also a *creative* one. Origami is great for kids who are still learning how to work together with others. Here, they each have their own papers, but can collaborate on their projects.

Learning to make origami also takes time, and it's a great way to help kids learn to *deal with mistakes*. If folds and creases aren't in the correct place, the origami may not work. That's OK, kids can practice learning to deal with a mistake, figuring out what to do next to fix it, or how to make it work.

On the next few pages, you'll find two beginner origami projects.

<u>Materials needed</u>: Origami paper or square paper

Origami Hopping Frog

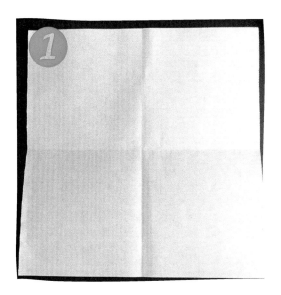

Fold paper in half
one way then
another, then open
up again.

Using the creases created
as markers, take top corner
and fold down to meet the
center lines on one side,
then the other.

Fold bottom of paper up to
meet the center line.

Fold half of the paper in to
meet the center line.
Repeat on the other side.

Fold bottom up along the crease.

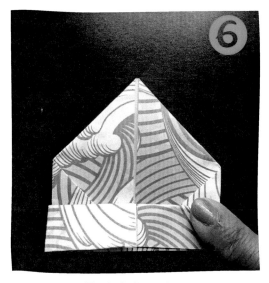

Fold back to meet the bottom of the paper

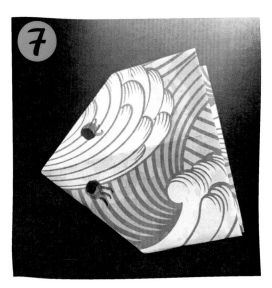

Flip over (and add eyes to your frog if you desire).

Place your finger on the back edge of the frog and move it back quickly to see it "hop"

Origami Twirly Birds

Turn the paper so it looks like a diamond

Fold paper in half, taking bottom corner to meet the top corner

Fold triangle in half then open back up again

Fold triangle in half the other way, with the corner of the triangle top going a little bit past the bottom of the triangle.

Fold in half

Fold one wing down, about ¼ of the length of that side. Then repeat on the other side.

Hold onto the bottom part of the twirly bird, push it through the air and let go to watch it twirl to the floor.

CHAPTER 3: COMMUNICATION PLAY

Our children are growing up in a world where they need to learn how to communicate both online and in real life. Given the extent to which technology is in our children's lives, they will absolutely need to learn how to communicate online in a safe and healthy way; however, that doesn't mean that face-to-face communication is less important than it used to be. In fact, now that online play has become more prevalent, our children need more practice with direct communication play these days.

Communication play uses words and gestures as the primary means of play (e.g. charades, telling jokes, play acting). These games and activities help kids practice those essential in-person communication skills including picking up on body language, listening to others, and having conversations. In addition, children also get to practice social skills like making decisions, following directions, and cooperation.

These games in this section are simple and don't require a lot of time or effort to set up. These are games that can be used as a transitional activity during a playdate, as you go from one activity to another. These are also great to use to help shift the focus if things aren't going as expected. If tensions are running high due to interpersonal conflict (i.e. the kids are starting to get frustrated or angry with each other), it might be good to step in and tell a joke or ask a silly question to break up the mood.

Ask Some Silly Questions

Age Range: 3 +
Mess Level: 1 out of 3
Indoor or Outdoor: Either!

Skill Highlight: By asking a question, listening to someone else answer, and then taking a turn to answer yourself, these questions are a great way to *encourage communication* and *practicing conversations.*

Materials Needed:
- Imagination!

Directions:
Kids ask each other silly questions and take turns answering. It's similar to would you rather, but allows for more open

ended discussions and answers. On the next page are a few to get you started, or you can make up your own. This can also be a fun way to learn more about your playdate partner.

Which cartoon character would you like to be? Why?

What's the grossest thing that has ever happened to you?

If you had 3 wishes, what would you wish for?

If you could design your own video game, what would it be like?

What would you do if you had $1,000,000?

If I were a grown-up, I would forbid...

If you were asked to sing on stage, what song would you pick?

If you had a time machine, when and where would you go?

If I were invisible, I would....

Describe your perfect day.

Quiz Each Other with "Would You Rather?"

Age Range: 5 +

Mess Level: 1 out of 3

Indoor or Outdoor: Either!

Skill Highlight: Besides making kids laugh, this game also helps them work on *making decisions*. When you play would you rather, you have to make a decision between the two items given.

Materials Needed:
- Imagination!

Directions:

This is one of my favorite games to play with kids when I need to pass time waiting in line, or in the car or at the dinner table. All it requires is a bit of imagination to come up with questions. It's a great way for kids to practice decision making, and explaining why they made their choice helps work on critical thinking skills. On the next page, you'll find 18 would you rather questions you can use to get started. Encourage inventiveness by having kids make up their own would you rather questions too!

Would You Rather…

be locked in an amusement park or a library?

Would You Rather…

change your eye color or change your hair color?

Would You Rather…

wear a uniform or choose your own clothes?

Would You Rather…

have to sew all your clothes or grow your own food?

Would You Rather…

eat chips or candy?

Would You Rather…

shoot spaghetti from your fingers or sneeze meatballs?

Would You Rather…

always have to enter rooms backwards or always have to somersault out?

Would You Rather…

have hands for feet or feet for hands?

Would You Rather…

live in the future or the past?

Would You
Rather…

be able to fly or
be invisible?

Would You
Rather…

live in the city
or on a farm?

Would You
Rather…

only eat foods
that begin with "b"
or only orange
foods?

Would You
Rather…

be limited to 500
words a day or
500 steps a day?

Would You Rather…

never be able to
sing or
have to sing
everything you
say?

Would You
Rather…

be a wizard
or
an elf?

Would You
Rather…

have an imaginary
jet or
a flying
broomstick?

Would You
Rather…

live with
Superman or with
Spiderman?

Would You
Rather…

have it snow
scoops of ice
cream or have it
rain apple juice?

Read or Make a Joke Book

Age Range: 5 +
Mess Level: 1 out of 3
Indoor or Outdoor: Indoor

Skill Highlight: This is another silly way to encourage working on those *communication skills*! Kids have to listen well in order to hear the punchline of the joke, and the joke teller has to make sure the other person is listening and deliver the punchline at the right time.

Materials Needed:
- Pencils or pens
- Paper

Directions:

A joke book can be great entertainment for kids together. They can read the jokes to each other, and have the other guess the punch line. They can also make up their own jokes. They can work on word puns too — which helps kids work on picking up on context clues to understand the joke.

Here are some simple jokes to get you started:

Q: Why did the chicken cross the road twice?
A: Because he was a double crosser!

Q: What did the bread say to the cheddar on picture day?
A: Say cheese!

Q: Why did the dog cross the road?
A: To get to the barking lot!

Q: Where do cows go for entertainment?
To the moo-vies!

Q: Knock Knock
A: Who's there?
Q: Snow
A: Snow who?
Q: It's snow use, I'll never run out of jokes!

Begin with the End

Age Range: 5 +
Mess Level: 1 out of 3
Indoor or Outdoor: Either!

Skill Highlight: In order to play this particular game, kids will work on their *listening skills*. They have to pay attention to the word that the person said, and then use that knowledge to take their turn.

Materials Needed:
- Imagination!

Directions:
This is a fun game that requires listening to the word the previous person said, then coming up with a word that starts with the letter they ended on.

Horse... Ear... Right...Tiger...

It's great for car rides, or waiting in restaurants, because all it requires is listening. Want a challenge? Make it more complex by limiting the categories, like only naming animals.

Play with Story Cubes®

Age Range: 8 + (but can be done with younger children too!)
Mess Level: 1 out of 3
Indoor or Outdoor: Indoor

Skill Highlight: To create a story that makes sense, the kids have to *work together*. They have to listen and build on one another's ideas to make a story that has a beginning, middle and end.

Materials Needed:
- A set of Story Cubes®

Directions:
This game requires some thoughtfulness and imagination to make up stories with images you've rolled on the dice. There

are several different versions of the game available, and it's always interesting to see what adventures people tell. Kids can practice taking turns while making up the stories.

Write Your Own Stories with Mad Libs™

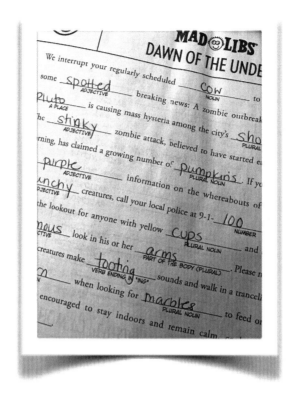

Age Range: 8 +

Mess Level: 1 out of 3

Indoor or Outdoor: Either!

Skill Highlight: This is a good opportunity to kids to practice *following directions* to fill in the Mad Libs to create the wacky story. Once it's all done, then you can read it out loud to find out how silly it really is.

Materials Needed:
- Mad Libs™ notepad
- Pens or pencils

Directions:

Mad Libs are a fun way for kids on a playdate to be silly together. One child has the mad lib, and asks the other child for words to put in without any context. Once the whole mad lib is filled in, then they can read the story out loud and giggles will follow.

There are also Mad Libs Jr, which are shorter and easier to fill in.

Mix Up Your Words

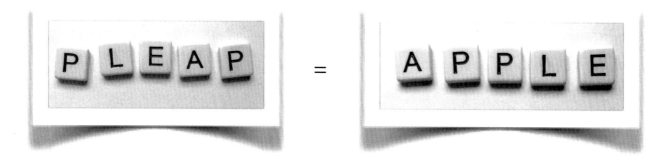

Age Range: 8 +
Mess Level: 1 out of 3
Indoor or Outdoor: Either

Skill Highlight: This is a fun way for kids to practice *flexible thinking*. They have to ignore the order the letters are given in and then try to figure out what other order works to make a word using all the letters.

Materials Needed:
 • Minds at work

Directions:
Take a simple word and mix up the letters. Then have the other person guess what the word is by un-mixing the letters.

You can do this verbally:
Person one says the three letters: C T A
Person two guesses: CAT?
Yes!

Or if it's a little too complicated to do orally, you can use letters from a game like bananagrams or magnetic letters or letter blocks.

The longer the words are, the harder it gets!

R P E O = ROPE

P L E A P = APPLE

CHAPTER 4: GET UP AND MOVE

Movement play means moving just because it's fun. Things like chase, tag, hide and seek, and tree climbing fall into this category. Movement is a powerful way for kids to play. Research that has been done on physical play shows that this kind of play can re-energize and reset a child's nervous system. This means that they are more able to concentrate on challenging tasks after a movement break, like recess.

Movement can also help kids with self-regulation. Peter Gray, Ph.D., who wrote the book <u>Free to Learn</u>, speaks about how rough-and-tumble play can help kids learn how to manage emotions, like fear and anger, and is a healthy part of social and cognitive development. The movement activities listed below work on social skills like problem solving, communication, taking turns, working together, understanding personal space, managing frustration, and patience.

While there are a lot of movement games that can involve groups of children, these ideas for moving are ones that can be done with just two, since that is the ideal place to start for kids who are building social skills and friendships. To give you even more ideas for movement play, there's also a list of over 20 two-player movement games, some of which can be played indoors, some outdoors.

Build an Obstacle Course

Age Range: 3 +

Mess Level: 2 out of 3

Indoor or Outdoor: Indoors or Outdoors

Skill Highlight: Obstacle courses allow for ample opportunities to work on *problem solving* skills. How will you set up the course? How do you balance an item? Can we fit through that space we've created? Have the kids start and see what problems arise, and how they can solve them.

They can do an obstacle course indoors or you can set up one outdoors, whichever works best for you and your space.

<u>Materials Needed</u>: These are just some ideas, you can use whatever you have on hand, indoors or out, to create an obstacle course:

- Jump Rope
- Plastic Cones
- Blocks
- Cups
- Chairs
- Gym Mat
- Scooter

Directions:

Have kids work together, use their imagination and create an obstacle course. Once it's all set up, see how fast you all can get through it. Then try a different set up and see how well you get through that one.

Play Balloon Tennis

This is a simple way for kids to practice taking turns and get a little movement in as well! If you want to add in a little arts and crafts fun to this project, have kids personalize their racket. They can decorate the paper plates and popsicle sticks before you start your balloon tennis game.

Age Range: 5 +

Mess Level: 1 out of 3

Indoor or Outdoor: Outdoor

<u>Skill Highlight</u>: In order to play a game of balloon tennis, you need to *take turns* and *work together* with your partner. You have to be paying attention to where the ball is hit, know where you need to get your body so that you can get the balloon back to your partner without it falling to the ground, and how much force you need to hit it back and forth, depending on how far apart you are standing from your partner.

Materials Needed:
- Paper Plates
- Big Popsicle Sticks
- Balloons

Directions:

Attach one popsicle stick to one paper plate. Make enough so that each child has one "racket". Then blow up balloons for the group to use as balls. See how many times they can hit the balloon before it touches the ground. Have them start close together as they get the hang of hitting the balloon. After a few minutes, have them take a step back away from one another and see if they can continue to hit the balloon back and forth. After a few more minutes, have them take one more big step back away from each other.

Set up a Game of Bowling

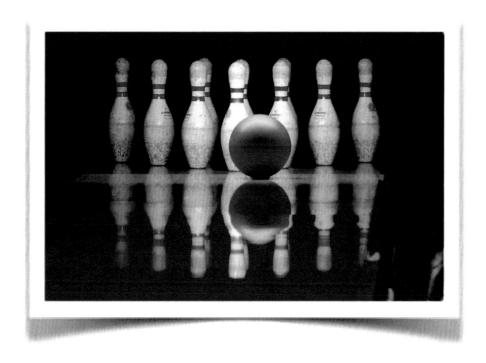

Age Range: 5 +
Mess Level: 1 out of 3
Indoor or Outdoor: Either

Skill Highlight: Bowling is a game where you can practice a little *patience*. If you're playing at home, you have to be patient and set up the pins again once a person's turn is over. It's also an opportunity to show *good sportsmanship* by being supportive while others are bowling.

Materials Needed:
- Bowling set
- Or cardboard + a small ball

Directions:

You can set up your own bowling game at home! There are small bowling sets you can purchase. Or if kids are feeling especially creative, they can make their own bowling set from cardboard and a small ball. Remember, if you play at home, you'll need to reset the pins yourself every time a person's turn is over.

Other Ideas for Movement Play

• Badminton	• See-saw
• Basketball	• Simple Races
• Bikes	• Skateboarding
• Catch	• Slackline
• Climb trees	• Skipping
• Frisbee	• Soccer
• Hopscotch	• Stomp Rockets
• Jump Rope	• Table Tennis
• Mini-Golf	• Tag
• Playground	• Taking a walk
• Rock Climbing – indoors or outdoors	• Trampoline – indoors or outdoors
• Roller Skating	• Zipline
• Scooters	

CHAPTER 5: PRETEND PLAY
Socio-Dramatic Play

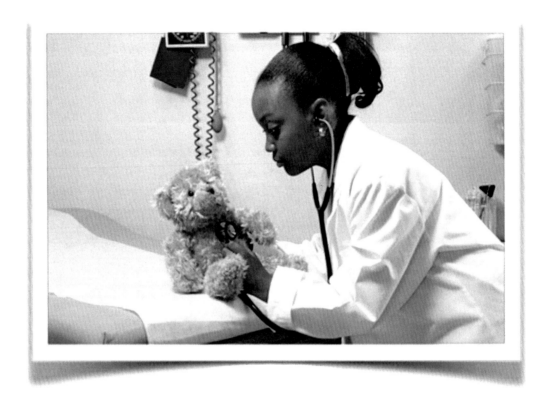

Age Range: 3 **+**

<u>Mess Level</u>: 2 out of 3

Indoor or Outdoor: Either!

<u>Skill Highlight</u>: Socio-dramatic play is the type of play that happens when children act out experiences, e.g. playing house, going to the shops or going to a restaurant. They get to try out different personalities and replay things in their life that they've seen the grown ups or older kids in their family or friends do. David Elkind, Ph.D., the author of <u>The Power of Play</u>, speaks about how trying out different roles during

pretend play helps kids see which ones fit their personality and temperament the best.

Also, by trying on these different roles, they work on social skills like *taking another person's perspective,* which will lead to practicing empathy. They also practice how to *solve problems* (what if everyone wants to be a cook when playing restaurant?) and the art of compromise. Research on preschoolers found that those who use this type of play frequently also have good emotional self-regulation.

Kids can also practice *executive functioning skills* when they're planning out their play.

 *A Quick Note:* Executive Functions are a set of skills that make it possible to set up goals, make a plan to meet those goals, and follow through until it is done. These skills include things like organizing and planning, paying attention, staying focused, thinking flexibly, and regulating emotions.

A great way to think about executive functioning is with the phrase "Ready, Do, Done."

Kids can use READY, DO, DONE with socio-dramatic play.

READY – Encourage kids to figure out what they want to play, and think through what they need on their own. They can then make a plan about who is going to do what

DO – Get started and play!

DONE – Clean up and put away all the materials that were used during playtime.

Materials Needed:

- See options on the next pages

Directions:

If they need an idea of where to get started, on the following pages are some ideas for play themes and items that could help. Remember, these are just starting points, they are not exhaustive lists. If this helps spark an idea for a different way to play, let them go and see what happens!

Suggested items that are in italics are printables available in this book for your convenience.

RESTAURANT	ART SHOP	MECHANIC SHOP
• *Menu* • *Order Form* • Pretend Food • Dishes, cups and flatware • Tablecloth	• Artwork to sell – have kids get creative and make things for the shop • *Order Form* • *Price Tags* • Cash Register	• Cars/Trucks • Tow truck to take cars to the shop • Cardboard boxes for cars to go in and get fixed • Cash Register
POST OFFICE/ UPS	**GROCERY STORE**	**VACATION**
• *Pretend Stamps* • Envelopes • Cardboard boxes of all shapes and sizes • *Pretend bar codes* • Scanner • Mail slot • Name tags	• Paper bags • Empty food containers from recycling or pretend food • Labels for sections of supermarket • *Price tags* • Cash register • Scanner for checkout	• Suitcase • *Passport* • Camera • Map • Postcards

Menu

Menu

Coffee   Tea

Hot Cocoa   Lemonade

Menu

Menu

Order Form

Order Form

Order Form

Order Form

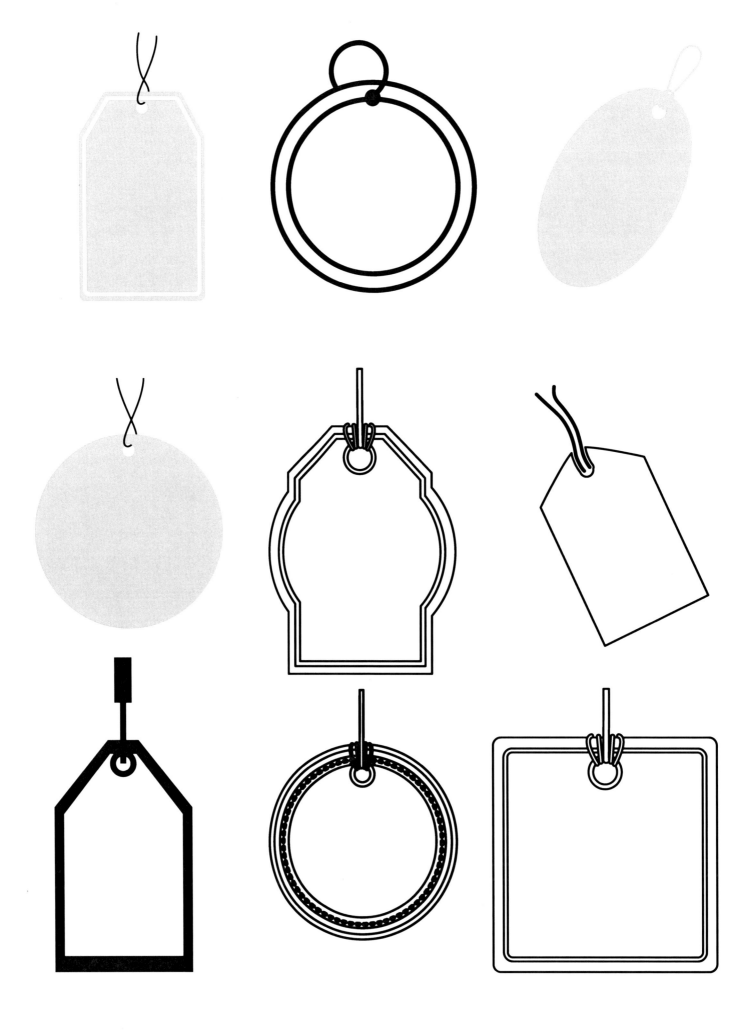

00 00 0000 000000

00 00 0000 000000

00 00 0000 000000

0 0000000000 000000

0 0000000000 000000

0 0000000000 000000

00000000000000

00000000000000

00000000000000

0000 000000000

0000 000000000

0000 000000000

PASSPORT

Imaginative Play

Dr. Tony Wagner, a well-known education advocate and expert, identified imagination as one of the seven skills crucial for 21st century kids.[1] According to Wagner, imagination is one of these essential skills because promotes innovation and the ability to solve problems creatively. Dr. Albert Einstein spoke about the power of imagination, as well, saying "Imagination is more important than knowledge."

Imaginative play is based on the principle that the conventional rules of our world do not apply. For instance, a

---

[1] The other skills are: critical thinking & problem solving, collaboration across networks & leading by influence, agility & adaptability, initiative & entrepreneurship, effective oral and written communication, accessing and analyzing information, and curiosity.

human child imagining they are a bee, or pretending to live underwater.

Age Range: 3 +
Mess Level: 2 out of 3
Indoor or Outdoor: Either!

Skill Highlight: Similar to socio-dramatic play, kids get a chance to practice *executive functioning skills* when they're planning out their play. They also learn *how to solve problems* and cooperate.

On the next page are some examples of play themes with ideas for materials to get kids started. Just as we did with socio-dramatic play, remember, these are just starting points, they are not exhaustive lists. If this helps spark an idea for a different way to play, let them go and see what happens!

A Quick Note: Often times, imaginative play includes "mashups," or multiple play themes happening at the same time. Two kids on a playdate can combine their ideas into a unique play theme that covers both of their interests. So, they may be playing superheroes along with knights. Or they may play magical detectives. The flexibility of imaginative play opportunities gives kids practice using and stretching their imaginations and working collaboratively.

PIRATES

- Eye patches
- Treasure box
- Pirate hats
- *Treasure map*
- Gold coins (cut out from stiff felt or wooden coins painted gold)

SUPERHEROES

- Capes
- Masks
- Cardboard cuffs

MAGICAL PLAY

- Wands
- Capes
- Pot for potions
- Ingredients to make potions
- Fabric

DETECTIVES

- Magnifying glass
- Hat
- Secret codes (you can use the one that's in this book!)
- Book to write down clues

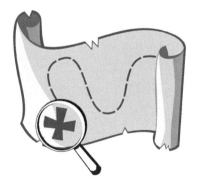

Play Dress Up

Age Range: 3 +
Mess Level: 2 out of 3
Indoor or Outdoor: Indoor

Kids love to dress up. You can make it open-ended by just having different items available, and see how they decide to play. Kids can put on a fashion show, or they can have you guess who they are, or just try on different personas depending on their clothes.

Skill Highlight: Dressing up gives kids a chance to walk in someone else's shoes and practice *seeing things from another person's perspective*. If they are creating stories to go along with their new outfits, kids get a chance to practice *executive functioning skills* when they're planning out their play. There may be conflicts over who will wear what, leading to teachable moments where kids can work on *solving problems* and *cooperating*. Some options for dress up include:

• Feather Boas	• Capes
• Hats	• Masks
• Clothes	• Vests
• Shoes	• Badges
• Jewelry	• Costumes

CHAPTER 6: OPEN-ENDED PLAY

Age Range: 3 +

Mess Level: 1 to 3 out of 3 (depending on what you choose!)

Indoor or Outdoor: Either!

Skill Highlight: In 1971, Simon Nicholson developed is a popular theory called "Loose Parts." He wrote a paper entitled "How **NOT** to cheat children". The "loose parts" he referenced are the materials that children can play with, and they can be used in a variety of ways to *encourage creativity*, experimentation and invention. This type of play is also perfect for practicing *flexible thinking* and for *seeing someone else's point of view*. The same materials/prompts can lead to very different creations.

There is no right or wrong way to engage in open-ended play. That's the beauty of setting out open-ended materials for children to use.

While it can be fun to set up materials (it's actually one of my favorite things to do - it's like I'm playing too!!), the goal is to have the child direct the play. You can do this by having the kids pick the materials or themes. They will be more invested in playing with things they get to pick out themselves.

Arts & Crafts Materials	Natural Materials	Other Materials
• Tissue Paper	• Stones	• Rubber Tires
• Foil	• Shells	• Containers of different sizes and shapes
• Yarn	• Pebbles	
• Fabric	• Twigs	• Buttons
• Markers	• Stumps	• Cardboard
• Q-Tips	• Logs	• Wood
• Play dough	• Sand	• Bottle caps
• Paint	• Water	• Cardboard Tubes
• Sequins	• Leaves	• Plastic Bottles
• Pipe Cleaners	• Seeds	• PVC Pipe
	• Flowers	• Rope
		• Chains
		• Paper Cups
		• Other items from the recycling bin

Here are a few different ideas for how to set up the materials:

Create a Tinker Tray

Set out several different materials and allow children to free play with it. You can give them a specific prompt ("Can you make a face with these materials or create a design using what you have in front of you?"), or you can leave it more open-ended. See how your child responds to both options.

I like using trays with several compartments and a cover because they can be easily stored and pulled back out again to use. And you can also easily change the materials out. If you run out of something, add another item that you have to that empty space.

Build an Invitation to Create

This is similar to the Tinker Tray, but more of a focused approach around a theme. Some examples are an invitation to create robots or or an invitation to create faces or an invitation to create art with leaves. You can set out related materials and see what they make.

For instance, if you wanted to make an invitation to create robots, you can put out paper shapes of different colors and sizes, cardboard, pipe cleaners, larger pieces of paper, googly eyes, metal brads, and glue and see what they create.

Build an Invitation to Play

This is similar to the invitation to create, but instead of creating something, kids are playing with the materials. You set out materials that fit a theme, and then you invite the kids to play and see what happens. Here are some examples of invitations to play:

- Fairies – small fairy figures, twigs, shells, smooth stones, and seeds
- Knights – knight figures, dragons, dragon eggs (marbles) and horses (see picture on the next page)

- Dinosaurs - toy dinosaurs, rocks, pretend trees, plastic easter eggs
- Outer Space - black play dough, tiny stars, sparkly pipe cleaners
- Superheroes - superhero figures, other figures, and blocks

You can have a space on a rug, a table, or in a tray for them to play. When you use a tray, you can also incorporate some sensory play by adding in different types of sand, water, play dough, water beads, or shaving cream - whatever you feel comfortable with the children using.

Set Out Open-ended Toys

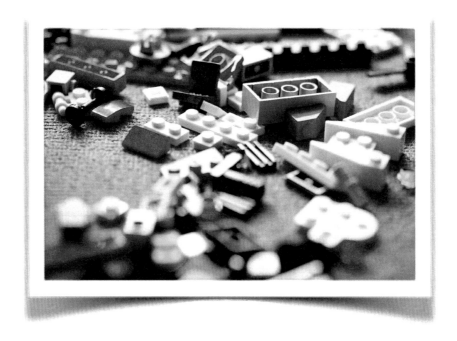

Using toys that are open-ended is a great way to make sure play sessions last longer. There are so many great toys that are versatile and kids find so many different ways to play with them.

What counts as an open-ended toy? Sometimes people may say that a toy that requires batteries or has buttons you push or lights up isn't open-ended. But that's not always the case. Whether or not a toy is considered open-ended has to do with how they play with it. One of my children's favorite toys to play with for years was a cash register. It had batteries and lit up, but they used it to play grocery store, or restaurant or mechanic shop.

On the other hand, they also had a toy table that had buttons that lit up and played songs when you pushed them. That was a toy they only played with in one way – press the button and listen to the song. Try to focus on toys that they can play with in different ways, which means they'll play with them longer, and they can be more creative in their playtimes.

Here are some ideas to get you started:

• Magna-Tiles	• Connectagons
• K'Nex (a variety box, not a set designed to create a specific item)	• KEVA® blocks
	• Marble Mazes
	• Small Figures
• LEGOs (the bricks, not a set designed to create a specific item)	• Pretend Food
	• Cash Register
	• Tents
• Toy Cars	• Play Dough
• Dolls/Stuffed Animals	• Blocks

CHAPTER 7: SOCIAL PLAY

Social play means any interactive activity where the expectation is that everyone will follow the same set of rules, like playing a single group game or making something together. In his book <u>The Power of Play</u>, David Elkind, Ph.D., writes about how social play helps children build social skills like cooperation, following rules, and good sportsmanship.

On the next pages are several activities where kids can make something together. In order to enjoy these activities, the kids need to organize themselves, make a plan, and follow through, utilizing *executive functioning* skills.

The other activities included in the section are cooperative activities where kids have to *work together* in order to do the activity. There are also ideas for board games and card games. By playing these games with structure and rules, kids work on strategy, observing others, as well as *winning and losing graciously.*

Experiment with Baking Soda & Vinegar

The reaction between baking soda and vinegar is bubbly and entertaining for kids to create. This activity allows for creativity and experimentation and making smart guesses about what will happen. This can be done indoors or outdoors, and depending on how much vinegar they use, the reaction can be somewhat big.

Age Range: 3 +
Mess Level: 3 out of 3
Indoor or Outdoor: Either, though outdoor would be better

Skill Highlight: These few simple materials can be used in so many ways – it's perfect to help kids practice *thinking flexibly*.

Materials Needed:
- Shallow pan of baking soda
- A small cup of vinegar for each child
- Eye droppers
- Food coloring/watercolors – optional

Directions:
Kids can take the eye-droppers and put a little vinegar in the baking soda and see what happens. What happens if they use more? What happens if they use less? Using food coloring or water colors adds even more to experiment with. What happens when I add in this color? What will happen if I mix these two? Let them experiment and figure out what happens!

Another way to play:
If they want to they can use playdough and make a volcano shaped creation in a pan with a hole in the middle of it. They can put baking soda in the bottom of the hole along with some red food coloring, then pour the vinegar in and watch the explosion take place. How fun!

Play with Cloud Dough, Oobleck, and Slime, Oh My!

Age Range: 3 +

Mess Level: 3 out of 3

Indoor or Outdoor: Outdoors or in the kitchen

Skill Highlight: By making these items, they work on *following directions*, and *executive functioning skills* in general. What materials do you need, what order do you need them in, and what are the steps you need to clean up after are all part of those essential executive functioning skills!

Materials Needed:

See recipes on the next page

Directions:

Choose one of these messy mushy substances to play with! Below are three simple recipes with only a few ingredients that you probably already have at home.

Cloud Dough
- 4 Cups Flour
- 1 Cup Oil

Oobleck
- Water
- Cornstarch

Slime with Contact Lens Solution
- 12 oz of Elmer's white glue
- 1 1/2 tablespoons Baking Soda
- 2 tablespoons of contact lens saline solution (or more, add as needed) Please note, the contact lens solution should have Boric Acid and/or Sodium Borate in order it to make the reaction to create slime.

Pull out a Puzzle

<u>Age Range</u>: 3 + (depending on puzzle complexity)
<u>Mess Level</u>: 1 out of 3
Indoor or Outdoor: Indoor

<u>Skill Highlight</u>: Working on a puzzle together is a great way to work on several social skills at once.

This is a perfect opportunity to practice organization and *executive functioning*. How do you start a puzzle? I like to start with the outer pieces to help give an idea of how big the puzzle is, where certain sections of the picture will be, etc. They can even divide out the puzzle pieces by colors or different areas of the puzzle to make it a bit easier to know what should go where.

Working on a puzzle also takes *patience*. It can take time to complete it, and maybe they won't finish it by the end of the playdate, but if there are more playdates planned, they can work on it more later.

Finally doing puzzles can help kids practice *flexible thinking*. Sometimes, you get convinced that an individual piece must go in a specific place, or go in a certain way. It's only after trying (and failing) that you realize that it doesn't fit that way, and you need to think differently.

Materials Needed:
- Large, flat surface on which to work
- Puzzle

Directions:
Make sure you select a puzzle that has all its pieces, and is age-appropriate for your playdate. Then get to work!

Go on a Nature Scavenger Hunt

Age Range: 3 +
Mess Level: 1 out of 3
Indoor or Outdoor: Outdoor

Skill Highlight: Doing a scavenger hunt helps kids *pick up on clues, think flexibly* ("could this be something fuzzy?" or "is this a treasure?") and *work together.*

Materials Needed:
- List of items
- Eyes and ears for looking!

Directions:

Encourage kids to go outside on their playdate by using a scavenger hunt. You can create your own, or use the one I created for you on the next page. If you use the nature scavenger hunt page, they could cross off the items they've found.

Remember, they don't have to find everything on one day. Maybe they mark when they've found something and the date, and continue to work on the scavenger hunt the next time they come over for a playdate.

Nature Scavenger Hunt

Two different
types of leaves

Something
brown

Spider's
web

Something
ROUGH

Drop of water

A flower

Something red

An Insect

A Rock

Moss

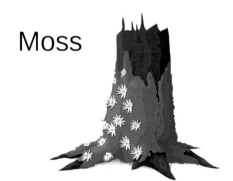

A Stick

Something
green

Something
SMOOTH

Something
FUZZY

A Treasure

Mirror Your Partner

Age Range: 3 +
Mess Level: 1 out of 3
Indoor or Outdoor: Either!

Skill Highlight: This is a game where kids mirror the actions of the other child. This activity helps kids *follow directions*, pay attention to what the other person is doing, and *take turns*.

Materials Needed:

- An open space to move around

Directions:

One child does an action, then the other one copies what they are doing as if they are their counterparts reflection in a mirror. Then the pair switches roles, so they each get a turn to be the leader. Encourage kids to make up their own and have fun. If they get stuck for ideas of what to do, on the next page are some to get them started!

If they're in the mood for a challenge, have them create a set of directions they have to follow. Create a series of steps starting with just one direction. Then add more directions on, and see how many steps they can remember. How many can they do and remember? Then rearrange the steps and start from the beginning.

Take 3 steps forward	Do 3 jumping jacks
Hop backwards once	Touch your knees
Wiggle your ears	Wrinkle your nose
Give yourself a hug	Stand on one foot
Put your hands on your head	Tap your toes
Put your hands on your hips	Stick out your tongue

Make a fishy face	Flap your arms like wings
Do a karate chop with your arms	Twirl like a ballet dancer
Hop like a bunny	Make a silly face
Pat your head and rub your belly	Wiggle your fingers and toes
Make circles with your arms	Jump as high as you can
Balance on your heels	Strike a silly pose

Break Out a Peaceable Kingdom® Board Game

Age Range: varies, see each game
<u>Mess Level</u>: 1 out of 3
Indoor or Outdoor: Indoor

Skill Highlight: All of the Peaceable Kingdom games are cooperative, which means all the players have to work together to win. What I love about these games is that it's a fun way to practice *cooperation* and *working together* and play a game at the same time. Often times, games can be quite competitive, but some kids really struggle with the competition part of games. This is a way they can practice following the rules, and *showing good sportsmanship*, but also be cooperative at the same time.

Janine Halloran

Materials Needed:

- Peaceable Kingdom game of your (or the kids') choosing

Directions:

Choose a game that works for your playdate. Here are some of the Peaceable Kingdom games we have played and loved!

Lemonade Shake Up

Ages 4 +. Players roll dice to complete lemonade orders to the customers at their lemonade stand. The goal is to work together to fill your jar up with 12 quarters before you get 4 sour lemons.

Hoot Owl Hoot

Ages 4 - 8. The goal is to get the baby owls in the nest before the sun rises. Players coordinate which colors to use to move the owls to get them to the nest. Such a cute game.

Catch!

Ages 6+. The players work together as cats to surround and catch the mouse before it reaches the fence; if they are successful, everyone wins!

Cauldron Quest

Ages 6 +. Players work together to find hidden ingredients to create a spell-breaking potion before all the pathways are blocked; if they do it, then everyone wins!

163

Mole Rats in Space

Ages 7 +. This game requires the mole rats to get their items into their spaceship without getting bitten by the snakes. Kids work together to identify which mole rats and snakes to move, and which items to gather next to avoid getting bitten. Once you've mastered the first set of cards, there's a harder expansion pack.

Play a Card or Board Game

<u>Age R</u>ange: 3 + (depending on the game)
<u>Mess L</u>evel: 1 out of 3
Indoor or Outdoor: Indoor

<u>Skill Highlight</u>: When playing a board game or card game, kids work on so many skills. They work on *taking turns* and *patience* as they play the game. They also work on paying attention to what's going on during the game, which is helpful when *making decisions* about what card to play or where to move next. Finally they also work on *good sportsmanship*, or learning how to win and lose graciously

165

Materials Needed: A variety of board or card games to choose from! Use what you have in your home, or ask your playdate buddy to bring over their favorite games.

Directions: There are a lot of great games that only require two players. Here are some ideas to get you started:

Board Games	Card Games
• Bounce off • Connect 4 • Checkers • Chess • Dominoes • Mancala • Jenga • Animal Upon Animal • Blokus • Shuttles • Yahtzee • Zingo • Hedbanz • Guess Who? • Trouble • Sorry • Battleship	• Crazy eights • War • Cribbage • Gin Rummy • Rummy 500 • Uno • Dos • Uno Flip

Make a Simple Snack Together

Age Range: 5 +
Mess Level: 2 out of 3
Indoor or Outdoor: Indoor

Skill Highlight: Being involved from beginning to end in making a snack helps kids learn to *follow directions*, and is a fun and tasty way to practice *executive functioning skills* like organization.

 *A Quick Note:* Children should have assistance from adults when in the kitchen. While none of these recipes require the stove, they do involve

using knives to cut up food. You know what your child is and isn't capable of, so use your best judgement when they are making a snack.

Also, make sure to check in regarding allergies and other dietary restrictions before making or serving anything.

Directions:
You can ask questions to help kids organize their thinking and planning:

- What do we need to get out to make our snack?
- What will we serve our food in/on?
- What should we do when we're done eating?

Apples with Cinnamon

- Apples
- Cinnamon
- Lemon juice (optional)

Cut up the apples into slices. Then sprinkle with cinnamon and serve immediately. To prevent apples from browning, squeeze lemon juice onto the apple slices before sprinkling with cinnamon

Yogurt with berries and granola

- Yogurt
- Berries (blueberries, cut up strawberries, blackberries, etc)
- Granola

Put some yogurt in a dish for each child, and let them add in the berries of their choice and a little granola. Enjoy the tasty snack!

Mini banana sandwiches
- Bananas
- Peanut Butter/Almond Butter/Sunbutter

Slice a ripe banana. Take one piece and spread peanut butter/ almond butter/sunbutter onto it, then place another piece on top. Continue until all banana slices are used.

Make Your Own Memory Game

Age Range: 5 +

Mess Level: 2 out of 3

Indoor or Outdoor: Indoor

Skill Highlight: When kids play memory, they have to work on *taking turns*. Another bonus of playing the game though is the opportunity to practice good sportsmanship, no matter whether you win or lose!

Materials Needed:
- Construction paper

- One bucket of colored pencils, markers or crayons
- Imagination!

Directions: Making the Game

There are tons of versions of Memory that you can find on the market. But if you want to make something truly unique, the kids can make their own memory game and play it.

1. Cut out 40 squares from the construction paper.

2. Draw the same image on two different pieces of construction paper. When you are done, you should have 20 pairs of images. You can keep it simple like squares, triangles, hearts, moons, suns. Or get more creative, drawing patterns or pictures. Be creative and have fun – just make sure both images look the same!

Directions: Playing the Game

1. Turn over all the squares – mix them up so the pairs aren't next to each other!

2. Decide who will go first.

3. Take turns trying to find the pairs. On your turn, turn over two squares. If the squares are the same, you keep the pair. If you find a pair, you get another turn. If you don't find a pair, it's your partner's turn.

4. **Keep going until all the pairs are found. The person with the most pairs wins!**

Playdates are a powerful way to create and build friendships. I've seen this first hand with children I've worked with, especially in schools. As a school counselor, I tried to look out for those kids who were struggling to make a connection. I looked for others who were interested in similar things, and tried to have them connect during lunch groups. Helping kids find those connections at schools was one of the best parts of my job, but my absolute favorite thing was when those bonds got stronger because their families were able to bring the kids together for playdates. When a child who was struggling to find a buddy finally connects with one or two people, it's like a whole new world opens up for them.

Recently, I did an interview about how to use playdates to build social and relational skills for children. Before we started recording, the interviewer told me about how her children made friends using playdates, and how they still are friends with some of those families today, and her kids are all grown up!

I've also seen the power of playdates with my own children. They still talk about fun times they had on playdates with friends. This is not to say that we should expect to be lifelong friends with every person we've ever had at our house for a playdate. Some connections last and some don't, that's typical and expected. But you may end up finding that family you just click with, which can be amazing.

Please remember that it's okay if a playdate doesn't go as expected. Don't give up just because it doesn't go well, or even if it's a full on disaster. Sometimes the best learning can happen when things aren't going well. The goal of having playdates is to get kids to have some positive interactions, and build up those friendship skills. Just keep going, and celebrate the small wins you see.

I know that scheduling and planning a playdate can feel overwhelming. And it may seem like the opposite of what you should do if your child is struggling with friendships and social interactions. I hope that this book has helped you understand that playdates are a natural way to practice social skills and build friendships. My hope is that this book makes it feel less overwhelming for you to take those steps and set up those playdates in a way that is helpful and supportive for your child.

Plus I hope your own creative juices have started to flow and you have come away with lots of simple ways to encourage play. Creativity thrives when it's encouraged. Give it a try, start small, and do the best you can. Once you start, you'll see more and more ideas come forward. Keep encouraging play and helping your child naturally build those skills. Happy playing!

APPENDIX A

Ten Activities with One or Two Supplies

Five Playdate Activities for Younger Kids

Five Playdate Activities for Older Kids

Playdate Activities by Social Skill

While all play will work on lots of different social skills at the same time, I've highlighted how certain activities can focus on a particular skill. See each activity for more details!

LISTENING

FOLLOWING DIRECTIONS

EXECUTIVE FUNCTIONING

TAKING TURNS

UNDERSTANDING PERSONAL SPACE

FLEXIBLE THINKING/THINK OUTSIDE THE BOX

PROBLEM SOLVING

UNDERSTANDING SOMEONE ELSE'S POINT OF VIEW

APPENDIX B: HELPFUL RESOURCES

Books for Parents / Caregivers

How to Make and Keep Friends
by Nadine Briggs and Donna Shea
They have a whole line of books to help kids, and this is where it all began. They give tips to help kids manage all sorts of social situations.

It's So Much Work to be Your Friend
by Richard Lavoie
This is a great book that has tons of information on how to support children who struggle socially.

The Happy Kid Handbook
by Katie Hurley
A fantastic book to help you figure out how to create a home that helps kids grow up well-rounded and develop positively.

Play: How it Shapes the Brain, Opens the Imagination and Invigorates the Soul by Dr. Stuart Brown with Christopher Vaughan
There are so many great quotes and wonderful information about the importance of play and its impact on our social lives. If you'd like to learn more about the important role play has across our lifespan, this is a great place to begin.

The Unwritten Rules of Friendship

by Natalie Madorsky Elman & Eileen Kennedy Moore

This is another great book for parents with some practical advice for understanding what's happening with their child and with some advice for what to do to help support them. It's divided into different personality traits/behavior characteristics (the shy child, the little adult) so you can just pick what you need to focus on and read that section.

Best Friends, Worst Enemies

by Michael Thompson, PhD and Catherine O'Neill Grace

This book is a thorough examination of children's social lives, from infancy through dating. The authors explore more specifics of how children develop friendships, manage and work through conflict, group dynamics, teasing and bullying.

Books with More Play Ideas / Inspirations

- The LEGO Play Book: Ideas to Bring Your Bricks to Life by Daniel Lipkowitz
- The LEGO Ideas Book: Unlock Your Imagination by Daniel Lipkowitz
- Super Sensory Invitations to Play by Cathy James
- C.R.A.F.T. Creating Really Awesome Free Things by Jamie Dorobek
- Playful Learning Lab for Kids by Claire Heffron and Lauren Drobnjak
- Great Big Book of Children's Games by Debra Wise

- <u>101 Kids Activities That Are the Bestest, Funnest Ever!: The Entertainment Solution for Parents, Relatives & Babysitters!</u> by Holly Homer and Rachel Miller

Books for Kids to Read for Inspiration

- <u>Not a Box</u> by Antoinette Portis
- <u>Not a Stick</u> by Antoinette Portis
- <u>Beautiful Oops</u> by Barney Saltzberg
- <u>What Do You Do With An Idea</u> by Kobi Yamada and Mae Besom
- <u>Snippets: A Story about Paper Shapes</u> by Diane Alber

Websites with Great Play Ideas

- Frugal Fun for Boys and Girls – frugalfun4boys.com
- Ideas for Origami – Origami-fun.com
- The Inspired Treehouse – theinspiredtreehouse.com
- Mad Libs – madlibs.com
- Mosswood Connections – mosswoodconnections.com
- Red Ted Art – redtedart.com or the Red Ted Art YouTube Channel

Academic Resources

Brown, S. L., & Vaughan, C. C. (2010). *Play: How it shapes the brain, opens the imagination, and invigorates the soul.* New York: Avery.

Dauch, C., Imwalle, M., Ocasio, B., and Metz, A. (2018). The influence of the number of toys in the environment on toddlers' play. *Infant Behavior and Development.* https://doi.org/10.1016/j.infbeh.2017.11.005

Elkind, D. (2018). *The power of play: Learning what comes naturally.* Vancouver, B.C.: Langara College.

Ginsburg, K. R. (2007). The importance of play in promoting healthy child development and maintaining strong parent-child bond, *Journal of American Academy of Pediatrics*, 119 (1), 183-185.

Hughes, B. (2002) *A Playworker's Taxonomy of Play Types, 2nd edition*, London: PlayLink.

Lavoie, R. D., Levine, M. D., Reiner, R., & Reiner, M. (2006). *Its so much work to be your friend: Helping the child with learning disabilities find social success.* New York: Simon & Schuster.

Mraz, K., Porcelli, A., & Tyler, C. (2016). *Purposeful play: A teachers guide to igniting deep and joyful learning across the day.* Portsmouth, NH: Heinemann.

Nicholson, S. (1971). How not to cheat children: The theory of loose parts. *Landscape Architecture*, 62, 30–35.

Parten, M. B. (1933). Social play among preschool children. *The Journal of Abnormal and Social Psychology, 28*(2), 136-147. doi:10.1037/h0073939

Reading, R. (2007). The importance of play in promoting healthy child development and maintaining strong parent–child bonds. *Child: Care, Health and Development, 33*(6), 807-808. doi:10.1111/j. 1365-2214.2007.00799_8.x

Robinson, K. (n.d.). Retrieved June 28, 2019, from https://www.ted.com/talks/ken_robinson_says_schools_kill_creativity

Singer, D. G., Golinkoff, R. M., & Hirsh-Pasek, K. (2010). *Play = learning: How play motivates and enhances childrens cognitive and social-emotional growth.* New York: Oxford University Press.

U.S.Cong. (1996). *The rights of the child* [Cong.]. Geneva, Switzerland: Centre for Human Rights, United Nations.

Tony Wagner's Seven Survival Skills. (n.d.). Retrieved from http://www.tonywagner.com/7-survival-skills/

Wenner, M. (2009). The Serious Need for Play. *Scientific American Mind, 20*(1), 22-29. doi:10.1038/scientificamericanmind0209-22

Made in United States
North Haven, CT
05 January 2023

30648801R00108